Feeling that none of the existing editions of *Ulysses* adequately represents the text of the novel, Philip Gaskell and Clive Hart have looked again at the evidence of Joyce's manuscripts, typescripts, and proofs, and have produced lists of suggested alterations for the three most important editions of the book: the first edition of 1922, the standard American edition of 1961, and the so-called 'corrected' edition of 1984. They believe that a copy of any of these editions, marked up with the alterations they propose, will result in a text closer to what Joyce intended in 1922 than any that has yet been achieved. What is offered here, in fact, is not a new edition of *Ulysses*, but a kit for repairing the major faults of existing editions.

This volume is the fourth in the Princess Grace Irish Library series.

ULYSSES
A REVIEW
OF THREE TEXTS

Princess Grace Irish Library: 4

THE PRINCESS GRACE IRISH LIBRARY SERIES
(ISSN 0269–2619)
General Editor: C. George Sandulescu

1. *Assessing the 1984* Ulysses. C. George Sandulescu & Clive Hart (editors)
2. *Irishness in a Changing Society.* The Princess Grace Irish Library (editor)
3. *Yeats the European.* A. Norman Jeffares (editor)
4. Ulysses. *A Review of Three Texts.* Philip Gaskell & Clive Hart

THE PRINCESS GRADE IRISH LIBRARY LECTURES SERIES
(ISSN 09050–5120)
General Editor: C. George Sandulescu

1. *The Parameters of Irish Literature in English.* A. Norman Jeffares
2. *Language and Structure in Beckett's Plays.* Clive Hart With *A Beckett Synopsis.* C. George Sandulescu
3. *Jonathan Swift and the Art of Raillery*, with *Notes on Irish Writers Associated with Swift.* Charles Peake
4. *Ireland and the Celtic Connection.* Glanville Price With *A Celtic Bibliography.* Morfydd E. Owen, edited by Glanville Price
5. *Joyce, Huston and the Making of* The Dead. Clive Hart
6. *Joyce, the Artist Manqué and Indeterminacy.* Morris Beja

ULYSSES

A REVIEW
OF THREE TEXTS

PROPOSALS FOR ALTERATIONS TO THE
TEXTS OF 1922, 1961, AND 1984

Philip Gaskell and Clive Hart

Princess Grace Irish Library: 4

BARNES & NOBLE BOOKS
Totowa, New Jersey

First published in the United States of America in 1989 by
Barnes & Nobles Books, Totowa, New Jersey 07512

Library of Congress Cataloging-in-Publication Data

Gaskell, Philip
 Ulysses: a review of three texts: proposals for
alterations to the texts of 1922, 1961, and 1984/
Philip Gaskell and Clive Hart.
   p. cm.
 ISBN 0-389-20874-4 (alk. paper)
 1. Joyce, James, 1882–1941. Ulysses–Criticism.
Textual.
 I. Hart, Clive. II. Title.
PR6019.09U645 1989
823'.912–dc20

89–34034
CIP

Produced in Great Britain
Phototypeset by Black Bear Press Limited, Cambridge
Printed in Great Britain by Dotesios Printers Ltd,
Trowbridge, Wiltshire

Contents

Abbreviations and References

1922   the first impression of the first edition of *Ulysses*, Shakespeare and Company, Paris 1922; references are to page and line numbers

1926   the first impression of the second edition of *Ulysses*, Shakespeare and Company, Paris 1926

1932   the first impression of the Odyssey Press edition of *Ulysses*, 2 vols, Hamburg 1932

1961   the first impression of the second Random House edition of *Ulysses*, New York 1961; references are to page and line numbers

1984   the critical and synoptic edition of *Ulysses*, ed. Hans Walter Gabler, 3 vols, Garland Publishing, New York and London 1984 (with corrections from the second impression, 1986); references are to line and word numbers (when separated by a point) or to episode and line numbers (when separated by a hyphen) of the clear text

aE   Joyce's autograph errata list (JJA 12 pp. 176–88)

Egoist *The Egoist*

HWG Hans Walter Gabler

J   James Joyce

JJA   *James Joyce Archive*, ed. Michael Groden, 63 vols, Garland Publishing, New York, 1977–9 (of which vols 12–27 concern *Ulysses*; see the Synopsis, below)

LR   *The Little Review*

MS   manuscript

OED *The Oxford English Dictionary*

P   primitive draft

ABBREVIATIONS

p1E   first printed errata list (JJA 12 pp. 203–216)

R   *Ulysses, a facsimile of the manuscript*, ed. Clive Driver, 3 vols, Rosenbach Foundation, Philadelphia and London 1975; references are to the foliation in the manuscript of the episode concerned

tE   typescript errata list (JJA 12 pp. 189–201)

TS   typescript

TN   textual note

We have gratefully used Ian Gunn and Alistair McCleery, *The* Ulysses *pagefinder*, Split Pea Press, Edinburgh 1988, which helped us to find our way quickly about the overlapping documents reproduced in JJA

Introduction

This book contains three sets of textual notes designed to enable the reader to make alterations to three important editions of *Ulysses:* the first edition (1922), the second Random House edition (1961), and the so-called 'Corrected Text' edited by Hans Walter Gabler (1984, revised printing 1986). We believe that a copy of any of these editions, marked up as we suggest, will offer a text closer to what Joyce intended in 1922 than does the Gabler edition. While the three marked-up texts will be almost identical in substance, the quality of their presentation on the page will be noticeably different. Although we have suggested changes to punctuation and spelling where these affect the sense, we have not tampered with indifferent variants, preferring to leave the tone of each edition in this respect unaltered.

We have not reedited *Ulysses*, nor do our suggestions amount, in aggregate, to a new edition. We have compiled our notes because of our dissatisfaction with some important aspects of the Gabler text, on which we nevertheless rely heavily. While we have not attempted to redo the decade of editorial work leading to its publication, we have considered each of the variants listed in the Historical Collation appended to 1984 and we have checked them as far as possible against facsimiles of the manuscripts, typescripts, and proofs. Despite our necessary reliance on facsimiles, we have sometimes disagreed with Gabler's readings. Our main source of dissatisfaction does not, however, arise from the comparatively small number of errors which, along with other users, we have found in Gabler's reporting of the bibliographical facts, but from a fundamental disagreement with his handling of the evidence and with his understanding of what it is desirable to present as a clear-reading text. We have, that is to say, only minor quarrels with the left-hand page of the three-volume 1984; it is with the right-hand page that we take issue.

We are troubled by three characteristics of the 1984 clear-reading text: (1) its preference for readings derived from the evidence, usually manuscript, of Joyce's first thoughts, however strong the case for later versions; (2) its normalisation of inconsistencies and errors even when these are indisputably attributable to the author; (3) most important:

the adoption of readings from sources, usually manuscript, that are not in the direct line of descent of the final text.

(1) The Gabler edition shows a strong preference for Joyce's first thoughts. Perhaps the most obvious example of this is the use Gabler makes of the primitive first draft (P) of Eumaeus. Although this chapter was linearly developed from P through R, typescripts, placards, and proofs, Gabler adopts twenty abandoned readings from P in place of the later revisions. Like all creative artists, Joyce revised as he wrote. Unexplained typed or printed variants in typescripts and proofs are regularly perceived by Gabler as transmissional errors to be editorially emended even when Joyce himself, while making other changes on the sheet, made no corrections to the passages in question. As it can never be demonstrated that Joyce approved such apparently inadvertent changes, 'passive authorisation' is excluded, on principle, from 1984. While the strength of such a principle is clear, there are times when it creates major problems. Whether or not Joyce wanted the changes which crept in, whether or not he would have corrected them had he noticed them at the time, these altered readings remained embedded in the text with which he continued to work. These were the readings that generated echoes and antitheses elsewhere in the book. The reestablishment of the superseded manuscript readings, however much more attractive they may sometimes be in isolation, destroys the network of interconnexions. This preference for first thoughts grows particularly noticeable in places where Joyce repaired mistypings and misprints. At such moments the Gabler edition conceives of Joyce as a fallible proofreader rather than as a fully alert artist. 'No, no, Mr Joyce,' it says, 'you are wrong here. What you really mean is . . .'. That kind of editorial private-secretaryship is in our view inadmissible. Not only does it verge on the impertinent to suggest that Joyce did not, at such moments, know what he was doing, but, even if he were to be supposed ready to accept the editorial advice, we believe that his later readings must be preferred. Those are the readings that became the basis for the further development of the text. They are, furthermore, the readings of an artist whose whole personality, whose whole being, including his potential fallibility in self-correction, is the generating force behind the book. Had Joyce been a careful proof-reader and a tireless checker of former drafts, had he been able to see better, had he not occasionally blurred his sight with excessive drinking, he would have written a book different in many important respects from *Ulysses*—from any version of *Ulysses*. The correction,

in the Gabler edition, of alleged oversights for which Joyce himself was responsible often results in an incoherent text, a text which is in effect an amalgam of two different versions of *Ulysses* written by two different largely incompatible Joyces. Even when no obvious incompatibility results, we think that any artist should be allowed his second thoughts, however inferior we may sometimes find them. If they are inferior, they are so because the artist is uneven. While the artefact ultimately displaces the artist, it ceases to be the work of the artist if it cannot be seen to have emerged from a single, developing, but always unified consciousness. It is not the editor's task to conflate what he deems to be the best products of the artist's creative activity to develop a superhuman work which could never have been engendered by any individual. While attempting to correct Joyce's alleged oversights, the Gabler edition often remains blind to the familiar way in which an artist will turn an inadvertency into a happy accident. Dr Kidd isolated a good example in Eumaeus: Joyce wrote about the 'blackguard type they had an insatiable hankering after (16–1805). The typist misread 'insatiable' as 'indubitable', which led Joyce to add to the typescript the word 'unquestionably', so creating a truly Eumaean tautology: 'blackguard type they unquestionably had an indubitable hankering after'. The additional word was, unquestionably, prompted by the mistyping (if mistyping it genuinely was). Gabler's restitution of 'insatiable' for 'indubitable' removes the point of Joyce's addition (which he of course includes).

(2) In similar vein, we believe that it is no business of an editor to act as post-factum amanuensis, checking and emending an author's idiosyncratic spellings and miscalculations, or expunging inconsistencies. Such oddities in the text are further products and expressions of the author's personality and training. They might be thought especially significant in *Ulysses*, where, as Joyce himself puts it in *Finnegans Wake*, so much else is set down 'with a meticulosity bordering on the insane' (FW 173.34). The Gabler text regularises many of Joyce's inconsistencies, and sometimes does so silently. In our list of suggested changes to 1984 we have not attempted to undo all such regularisations, but in our emendations to the other texts we usually leave mispellings and oddities of expression which can be shown to be authorial and which do not seem to be purely mechanical. These include a few words that are almost certainly oversights, such as 'homilectic' (17–752), and a few nonce-forms influenced by Joyce's domicile in foreign countries, such as 'pelosity' (17–1202). Sometimes

Gabler also corrects what he deems to be errors of fact (or at least of appropriate diction). Thus, to take a familiar example, he replaces Joyce's 'Roman indication' (17–89) with 'Roman indiction'. Perhaps Joyce, copying from Thom's Directory, meant to use the correct form for the fifteen-year cycle, of which he would have been fully aware. Perhaps it was a slip of the pen; but, again, perhaps not. We see no reason to change what Joyce very clearly set down.

(3) There are passages in the manuscripts—mainly in the Rosenbach manuscript, but occasionally also on proof—where Joyce made changes which he did not later use because the documents in question were set aside and did not form a link in the chain of descent of the final text. The readings on such end-stopped, branching documents are often interesting and in some cases we judge them to be, from a literary point of view, decidedly superior. As they did not, however, find a place in the text which Joyce subsequently developed, they belong to another, slightly different *Ulysses* which was never written and which must not, we believe, be confused with the version of 1922. For example, we retain the linear typescript reading 'mumbled sweet and sour with spittle' rather than adopt the more lyrical and perhaps more Bloomian Rosenbach reading 'mumbled sweetsour of her spittle' (8–908).

Gabler's insistence on the distinction between composition and transmission leaves little room for the effects on composition of the physical nature of the printed object. However poor a proofreader Joyce may sometimes have been, he was more than usually interested in the physical presentation of his books. His growing (and finally almost total) dislike of hyphens, his almost lifelong avoidance of quotation marks, his care to get the colour of the cover of *Ulysses* right are among the better known examples. The first edition, of 1922, was the physical object towards which Joyce consciously worked during the last stages of composition. He personally oversaw it and, although he failed to notice many misprints which it would be perverse to suppose had passive authorial approval and which we have accordingly followed Gabler in emending, he did not express general reservations about some important characteristics of the presentation of 1922 which were not adopted in 1984: e.g., the normal continental indentation of speech-dashes, the bolder, heavier type used for the cross-heads in Aeolus, and perhaps most especially, the heavier punctuation of Eumaeus, the pedantry of which we think Joyce probably grew to like and which he allowed to continue into print.*

The general appearance and tone of 1922, including, we would say, its punctuation, cannot have failed to influence the final stages of Joyce's work on the text. The lists of errata which Joyce drew up after the publication of the first edition include emendations of a number of minor errors, largely to do with spelling and punctuation, which Joyce evidently found disfiguring. We have incorporated these and a number of analogous changes in our lists, along with emendations of obvious typographical errors, but have otherwise attempted to preserve (in our list for 1922) the presentational character of the first edition, as overseen by Joyce, even when that differs from the extant authorial documents. There are, inevitably, a few instances where we have not been able to resolve our doubts. The first edition and its derivatives have, at 11–419, 'drankoff', emended by Gabler to 'drank off'. Although we are not sure that 'drankoff' is a word, even in Sirens, we have thought the issue undecideable and have therefore let each edition retain its reading. We are similarly in doubt about the repeated 'round' at 13–1161: 'lifebelt round round him'. This is deleted by Gabler on the grounds that it is a typist's erroneous repetition of R's single 'round'. While that may well be so, we find the repetition not incompatible with Bloom's tiring control of language at this point in Nausicaa and have accordingly decided to retain the reading of 1922.

The 1961 Random House edition, replacing but similar in physical presentation to the defective first American edition of 1934, was intended to be a faithful copy of 1922, with the errors corrected. Since it was the fifth successive transcript from 1922, it had accumulated almost as many new copying errors as it had emended old ones. Our lists of suggested changes repeat the emendations list for 1922, where these have not been corrected, and add necessary new corrections of substantive errors. We have decided not to bother the reader with minor presentational changes such as styles of abbreviation and word-division, typographical layout, and the occasional inadvertent American spelling, which have little or no affect on the sense of the book. Users of 1961 should nevertheless be warned that it exists in more than one state, with minor substantive variants (e.g., at 207.40, the erroneous 'sun' in the first printing has in later printings been corrected to 'son').

---

* Apart from inserting the ellipses for which Joyce clearly asked, we have not attempted to undo Gabler's editing of the punctuation in Eumaeus and have left 1984 with its lighter style to serve as an interesting variant.

INTRODUCTION

Our general editorial principle has been to adopt those substantive readings that are to be found in the direct line of transmission of the text. While we believe that this generates versions of *Ulysses* closer to the ideal than do Gabler's principles, we do not pretend that it will result in a definitive text, and on a few occasions we have in any case felt obliged to make decisions on more pragmatic grounds. Sometimes the transmitted version produces manifest nonsense while elsewhere a restoration results in a persuasive clarification of an obscurity or removes an uncharacteristic infelicity. Many small points must, furthermore, remain permanently in doubt. A pair of examples, from Nestor, may suffice. For the first edition's 'tangled' in 'His tangled hair and scraggy neck' (2–124) and 'lean neck and tangled hair' (2–139) Gabler substitutes, on both occasions, 'thick', a reading to be found in the early publication of the chapter in *The Little Review*. Although evidence for Joyce's authorisation is lacking, Gabler suggests that 'the identical change in two instances supports the authority of the revision' (1984, p. 1730). We have chosen to revert to the reading of 1922, supported by R, while believing that there is much to be said for yet a third version of the passage, suggested by Charles Peake:

I think it likely that Joyce wanted the LR printer to get rid of the repetition of 'tangled'. But the two places, though so close, are significantly different. In the first, Sargent's hair and neck 'gave witness of unreadiness': 'tangled' gives such witness, 'thick' does not. Moreover, between the two occurrences, Stephen has begun to feel a certain pity for the boy: 'tangled' and 'scraggy' are pejorative adjectives: 'lean' and 'thick' are not. The most likely explanation is that Joyce asked LR to replace the second 'tangled' by 'thick' and that due to some misunderstanding, both were changed. Critical argument here seems to me to favour strongly 'tangled hair and scraggy neck' . . . while accepting the LR emendation 'lean neck and thick hair'.*

Editorial judgement must also be exercised in passages such as Myles Crawford's hectic description of the flight of the Invincibles. At 7–669 he says 'X is Davy's publichouse in upper Leeson street'. 'Davy's' here had originally read 'Burke's' but was changed by Joyce on the typescript. Three lines further down Crawford (as represented in 1984) repeats himself: 'X is Davy's publichouse, see?' (7–672). In the typescript the second 'Davy's' had also read 'Burke's' but at this point Joyce made no change and the word was accordingly printed 'Burke's'

---

* Charles Peake, 'Some Critical Comments on the Telemachia in the 1984 *Ulysses*', *Assessing the 1984* Ulysses, ed. C. George Sandulescu and Clive Hart (Gerrards Cross 1986) 165–66.

in all editions before 1984. Was this an oversight by Joyce, or is the contradiction a deliberate indication of the crazed nature of Crawford's mind? Although after much thought we have chosen to reject Gabler's emendation and to read 'Burke's' on the second occasion, thus reproducing the contradiction that Joyce left in the typescript, the decision could easily go the other way.

A finely balanced example is found in Mulligan's reference to the lunatic asylum: 'He's up in Dottyville with Connolly Norman' (1–28). The common spelling 'Connolly', adopted by Gabler, is unique to R. The less common but in this case, historically correct spelling, 'Conolly', which appears in all printed documents, may, as Gabler argues, have been an unintended variant introduced into the missing typescript, but we think it as likely to have been Joyce's correction of an initial oversight in R. As the point cannot be clearly decided, we have suggested no alterations to any of the editions.

A related problem arises from the handling of a few substantive changes to the text which were introduced after the publication of the first edition. At the start of Scylla and Charybdis, Stephen refers, in 1922, to 'Monsieur de la Palice' (9–16). The historically incorrect spelling, as set down in R, is changed in the 1926 edition to the correct 'Monsieur de la Palisse'. This can hardly be an error in the same category as the scores of minor typographical blunders to be found in that poorly printed edition. Is it authorial, or is it perhaps a French printer's automatic correction of what he well knows to be a mistake? In common with Gabler, we have retained the unexplained reading that persisted in the direct line of descent up to the first edition, though we do so with some misgiving.

We have deleted from 1984 the famous passage about love in Scylla and Charybdis (9–426ff.). Although it appears in R (which is non-linear for this chapter), it is not in the typescript, the omission being, in Gabler's judgement, the result of an eyeskip in the transcription of the lost final working draft. As the typescript version is in the line of descent and was the basis for the placards and proofs which Joyce saw through to the publication of the first edition, we have, as in all similar cases, omitted the passage. From our point of view, that should perhaps be an end of the matter, but since it prompted so much discussion, we offer our own comment. Whatever the reasons for Joyce's failure to restore it, we do not agree with Richard Ellmann's view that 'it is most uncharacteristic of Joyce, so reticent about love, to allow Stephen to ask his dead mother a question to which he has already given the answer'.* Not only is repetition across wide textual gaps an important structural principle of *Ulysses*, but the comparability of this passage with Bloom's later highly charged argument in Cyclops establishes just the kind of parallelism between the two men which Joyce was at pains to develop. The omission, if authorial, was probably prompted by other motives.

The first draft of the list was produced by Philip Gaskell, the first draft of the Introduction by Clive Hart. Thereafter we have collaborated at all points. Each list gives, in the left column, the line.word number for the 1984 clear-reading text, followed, in the centre column (for 1922 and 1961), by the relevant page.line number. The alterations for 1984 are briefly annotated, but we have not thought it necessary to offer explanations for the changes to the earlier texts (which are annotated, explicitly or implicitly, in 1984). Readers interested in pursuing these matters further will find references either in the annotations to our 1984 lists or in the apparatus to 1984 itself. The list for 1922 contains 1697 entries; the list for 1961, 1584 entries; the list for 1984, 483 entries. Of the 483 alterations to 1984, 312 are the result of preferring TS to non-linear R in episodes 4–9, 11, 13, and 14; and a further 20 are the result of preferring R to P in episode 16. This leaves 151 alterations to 1984 which involve particular disagreements with Gabler.

P.G.
C.H.
July–December 1988

* Richard Ellmann, 'A Crux in the New Edition of *Ulysses*', *Assessing the 1984* Ulysses, 33.

Synopsis of JJA 12–27

Volume	Contents	Episodes
12	MSS and TSS plus notes, schemas, and errata lists	1–9
13	MSS and TSS	10–13
14	MSS and TSS	14–15[1]
15	MSS and TSS	15[2]-16
16	MSS and TSS	17–18
17	placards	1–6
18	placards	7–10
19	placards	11–14
20	placards	15–16
21	placards	17–18
22	page proofs	1–6
23	page proofs	7–9
24	page proofs	10–11
25	page proofs	12–14
26	page proofs	15
27	page proofs	16–18

ALTERATIONS TO 1922

1 : Telemachus

6.11	3.6	**for** called up coarsely: **read** called out coarsely:
8.8	3.7	**for** fearful Jesuit. **read** fearful jesuit.
24.9	3.22	**for** long low whistle **read** long slow whistle
24.12	3.22	**for** call then **read** call, then
86.5	5.19	**for** his great searching **read** his grey searching
127.13	6.22–3	**for** Mulligan says **read** Mulligan, says
128.13	6.23–4	**for** Norman. Genera paralysis **read** Norman. General paralysis
194.7	8.12	**for** and I went **read** and went
245.13	9.26–7	**for** harpstrings merging **read** harpstrings, merging
248.9	9.29	**for** slowly, shadowing **read** slowly, wholly, shadowing
249.5	9.30	**for** lay behind him, **read** lay beneath him,
250.3	9.30–9.31	**for** it above in **read** it alone in
255.5	10.1	**for** fans, tassled dancecards, **read** fans, tasseled dancecards,
258.3	10.3–4	**for** the pantomine of Turko the terrible and **read** the pantomime of *Turko the Terrible* and
314.5–7	11.26	**for** briskly about the hearth to and fro, hiding **read** briskly to and fro about the hearth, hiding

3

340.7–8	12.17	**for** said. There's **read** said thirstily. There's
349.1	12.24	**new paragraph at** He hacked
385.1–10	13.22–3	**insert para** He crammed his mouth with fry and munched and droned.
393.1	13.30	**insert dialogue dash**
417.1–6	14.19–20	**insert paragraph** – Look at that now, she said.
421.11	14.23	**for** likeness the **read** likeness, the
428.16	14.29–30	**for** from west, **read** from the west,
442.13	15.6–7	**for** at two pence is **read** at twopence is
444.8–10	15.8	**for** shilling and **read** shilling. That's a shilling and
490.4	16.15	**for** make money **read** make any money
515.11	17.3	**delete** Agenbite of inwit.
525.1	17.12	**begin new paragraph at** Resigned he
547.9	17.34	**for** made to **read** made out to
553.7	18.3	**for** said aimiably. Is **read** said amiably. Is
581.3	18.30	**for** suddenly withrawn all **read** suddenly withdrawn all
602.9	19.15	**for** brief birdlike cries. **read** brief birdsweet cries.
638.3	20.19	**for** am the servant **read** am a servant
666.6	21.10	**for** Britisher, Haine's voice **read** Britisher, Haines's voice
694.1–2	21.36–7	**for** and breastbone. **read** and lips and breastbone.

700.12   22.7   **for** is rotten with **read** is rotto with

2: Nestor

3.2   24.3   **for** Very good, Well? **read** Very good. Well?

24.2   24.23–4   **for** the tissues of **read** the tissue of

32.11   25.5   **for** the waves. A **read** the water. A

32.15   25.5–6   **for** of bridge. **read** of a bridge.

59.2–3   25.32   **for** the history, sir? **read** the story, sir?

64.5   26.1   **for** *woful shepherd, weep* **read** *woful shepherds, weep*

108.1   27.11   **delete indent**

186.5   29.15   **for** came stepping **read** came away stepping

190.11   29.19   **for** Stephen cried. **read** Stephen said.

197.6   29.26   **for** garish sushine bleaching **read** garish sunshine bleaching

210.5   29.37   **for** table strapping and **read** table.

242.13–14   30.31–2   **for** poet. but **read** poet, yes, but

252.1   31.4   **for** Goood man, **read** Good man,

259.2   31.10   **for** weeks' borard. The **read** weeks' board. The

266.9   31.18   **for** tartan fillibegs: Albert **read** tartan filibegs: Albert

269.10–12   31.20   **for** famine. Do **read** famine in '46. Do

275.3   31.26   **for** the planters covenant. **read** the planters' covenant.

287.1	32.1–2	**for** Soft, day, **read** Soft day,
306.1	32.20–21	**for** this important **read** this allimportant
309.3–310.3	32.24	**for** slush. Even money Fair rebel: ten **read** slush. *Fair Rebel! Fair Rebel!* Even money the favourite: ten
368.2	34.9–10	**for** eyes bellied the **read** eyes belied the
371.9	34.13	**for** knew the years **read** knew their years
379.5	34.22	**for** gave a you **read** gave you
380.14	34.23	**for** All history **read** All human history
404.1	35.10	**delete dialogue dash**
441.2	36.12	**for** sir, Stephen **read** sir? Stephen

3: Proteus

4.6	37.4	**for** diaphane But **read** diaphane. But
8.9	37.8	**for** fingers throught it, **read** fingers through it,
17.5	37.17	**for** the end of **read** the ends of
19.9	37.19	**for** money. Dominic Deasy **read** money. Dominie Deasy
23.7	37.22	**for** hear. A catalectic tetrameter **read** hear. Acatalectic tetrameter
24.1	37.22	**for** iambs march ing. No. **read** iambs marching. No.
55.3	38.30	**for** romped around him, **read** romped round him,
79.3–8	39.16	**after** nephew. **add** Sit down and take a walk.

92.6	39.28	**for** law. Harry **read** law Harry
95.4–6	39.31	**for** nowhere put toit, you **read** nowhere to put it, you
107.11	40.6	**for** bay, of **read** bay of
113.2	40.11	**for** dean what **read** dean, what
116.2	40.14	**for** monstrance, basliskeyed. Get **read** monstrance, basiliskeyed. Get
134.3–4	40.32	**for** *women!* What **read** *women! naked women!* What
135.4	40.33	**for** what? what **read** what? What
141.4	41.2	**for** epiphanies on **read** epiphanies written on
141.9	41.2	**for** leaves, deeeply deep, **read** leaves, deeply deep,
151.2–152.3	41.10	**for** breath. He **read** breath, a pocket of seaweed smouldered in seafire under a midden of man's ashes. He
194.4	42.14	**for** pintpots, loudlatinlanghing: *Euge!* **read** pintpots, loudlatinlaughing: *Euge!*
199.1	42.18	**for** Mother dying **read** Nother dying
212.11	42.31	**for** her hands. In **read** her hand. In
213.4	42.35	**for** newmake there tumbled **read** newmake their tumbled
215.8	42.37	**for** their well pleased **read** their wellpleased
220.5,10	43.4,5	**for** *Irlandais.* [...] *Irlandais,* **read** *irlandais.* [...] *irlandais,*
227.8–228.4	43.12	**for** now. To **read** now, AE, pimander, good shepherd of me. To
236.1–2	43.19	**for** *messieurs* not **read** *messieurs.* Not

242.10	43.26	**for** veil orangeblossoms, **read** veil, orangeblossoms,
249.2	43.32–3	**for** Shatte-/red **read** Shatter-/ed
289.3	44.32–3	**for** And there, the **read** And these, the
326.16	45.34	**for** of sands quickly **read** of sand quickly
358.6	46.27	**for** lifting his **read** lifting again his
360.2	46.28	**for** scattered sand: **read** scattered the sand:
374.5	47.5	**for** feet. A bout her **read** feet. About her
378.5	47.9	**for** in rogue's rum **read** in rogues' rum
402.1	47.31–2	**for** her womb. Oomb, **read** her moomb. Oomb,
404.1	47.33–4	**for** roaring wayawayawayawayawayaway. Paper. **read** roaring wayawayawayawayaway. Paper.
405.6	47.35	**for** for hospitality **read** for the hospitality
440.7	48.33	**for** *bona.* Alo! *Bonjour,* **read** *bona.* Hlo! *Bonjour,*
451.9–12	49.7	**for** name. He **read** name. His arm: Cranly's arm. He
457.4	49.13	**for** rsseeiss ooos. **read** rsseeis, ooos.
473.5–11	49.29	**for** bobbing landward, a pace a pace a porpoise. **read** bobbing a pace a pace a porpoise landward.
474.5	49.30	**for** quick. Sunk **read** quick. Pull. Sunk

4: Calypso

15.1	53.13	**begin new paragraph at** The cat
27.11–28.10	53.25,54.3	**transfer** Cruel. Her nature. Curious mice never squeal. Seem to like it. **from 54.3 to 53.25 following** Vindictive too. **and delete new paragraph**
36.1	54.8	**for** dresser took **read** dresser, took
53.1	54.25	**for** – I am going **read** – I'm going
73.6–7	55.7	**for** off must **read** off. Must
76.1–2	55.9–10	**for** over rhe threshhold, a **read** over the threshold, a
85.4	55.19	**for** sun steal **read** sun, steal
87.10	55.21	**for** moustaches leaning **read** moustaches, leaning
90.1	55.23	**for** crosslegged smoking **read** crosslegged, smoking
91.6	55.25	**for** sherbet. Wander along **read** sherbet. Dander along
93.2	55.26	**for** mosques along the **read** mosques among the
95.2	55.28	**for** watches from **read** watches me from
127.2	56.21–2	**for** the country Leitrim, **read** the county Leitrim,
136.2	56.31	**for** Joseph's, National **read** Joseph's National
141.5	56.36	**for** white. Fifty multiplied **read** white. Fifteen multiplied
142.1	56.37	**for** mind unsolved: **read** mind, unsolved:
144.4	57.2	**for** spicy pig's blood. **read** spicy pigs' blood.

147.7	57.5	**for** hand. Chapped: **read** hand? Chapped:
154.3–5	57.12	**for** took up a page from **read** took a page up from
178.7	57.35	**for** in Eccles' Lane. **read** in Eccles Lane.
195.2	58.14	**for** pay eight marks **read** pay eighty marks
200.2	58.20	**for** doing Still **read** doing. Still
218.7–8	58.37	**for** sun wholly slowly wholly. **read** sun slowly, wholly.
220.12	59.2	**for** wind would lift **read** wind could lift
230.5	59.11	**for** his ftesh. Folding **read** his flesh. Folding
231.3	59.12	**for** into Eccles' Street, **read** into Eccles Street,
243.8	59.23	**for** on ihe hallfloor. **read** on the hallfloor.
244.6	59.24	**for** His quick heart **read** His quickened heart
274.1	60.14–15	**for** kettle and crushed **read** kettle, crushed
302.5	61.9	**for** were? she **read** were, she
344.8	62.14	**for** mocking eye. The **read** mocking eyes. The
359.9	62.28	**for** watching its flow **read** watching it flow
361.3	62.30	**for** my garantor. Reincarnation: **read** my guarantor. Reincarnation:
362.9	62.31	**for** go on on living **read** go on living
400.7	63.30	**for** writing, They **read** writing. They
409.13–14	64.4	**for** respects. Must **read** respects. I must
445.1	65.4	**for** Reading lying **read** Reading, lying
447.3	65.5	**for** qualm regret, **read** qualm, regret,

450.4	65.8	**for** kissing kissed. **read** kissing, kissed.
519.3–4	67.4	**for** proverb which? **read** proverb. Which?
524.10–11	67.9–10	**delete new paragraph and run on** Rubbing smartly **following** her boot.
525.5	67.10	**for** her stocking calf. **read** her stockinged calf.
529.14	67.15	**for** good smell **read** good rich smell

5: Lotus Eaters

2.7	68.2	**for** linseed crusher's, the **read** linseed crusher, the
11.12	68.11	**for** the undertaker's. At **read** the undertaker. At
12.10	68.12	**for** bagged that job **read** bagged the job
16.1	68.15	**for** a whatyoumay call. With **read** a whatyoumaycall. With
27.12–28.12	68.27	**for** over again: **read** over his brow and hair. Then he put on his hat again, relieved: and read again:
32.3	69.4	**for** lobbing around in **read** lobbing about in
38.1–2	69.9	**for** Ah, in **read** Ah yes, in
41.1–2	69.12	**for** the. Or **read** the what? Or
61.4	69.32	**for** thanked and **read** thanked her and
66.1	70.1–2	**for** revie-/wing **read** review-/ing
93.7	70.28	**for** badge maybe **read** badge maybe.
118.8	71.15	**for** he fostering over **read** he foostering over

126.4	71.23	**for** *him*, he **read** *him?* he
156.6	72.16	**for** man. Cat **read** man. Letter. Cat
161.2	72.21	**for** *Comes lo-ve's old ...* **read** *Comes lo-ove's old ...*
187.1	73.13–14	**for** diffe-/rence? **read** differ-/ence?
195.1	73.21	**for** Mrs Bandman Palmer. **read** Mrs Bandmann Palmer.
195.7–9	73.22	**for** in that again. **read** again in that.
197.10	73.24	**for** talk about Kate **read** talk of Kate
203.1	73.29	**delete dialogue dash**
207.6	73.33	**for** glad. I **read** glad I
208.13	73.34	**for** was the best **read** was best
323.13–326.2	77.8–10	**transfer** Prayers for the conversion of Gladstone they had too when he was almost unconscious. The protestants the same. Convert Dr William. J. Walsh. D.D. to the true religion. **to 77.6 following** African mission **and add full stop after** mission
325.3	77.9	**for** protestants the **read** protestants are the
325.8	77.10	**for** William. J. **read** William J.
329.10	77.12	**for** Ecce Home. Crown **read** Ecce Homo. Crown
334.5	77.16	**for** specs whit the **read** specs with the
352.8–9	77.33	**for** corpse why **read** corpse. Why
390.8	78.34	**for** it: show wine: **read** it: shew wine:
423.1	79.29	**for** mass? Gloria and **read** mass? Glorious and

453.3	80.22	**for** time. Woman enjoy **read** time. Women enjoy
455.5–456.1	80.22–3	**transfer** Annoyed if you don't. Why didn't you tell me before. **to 80.24 following** the moon.
458.2	80.26	**for** into rhe light. **read** into the light.
473.3	81.4	**for** have, Shrunken **read** have. Shrunken
478.7	81.9	**for** Doctor whack. He **read** Doctor Whack. He
501.11–13	81.31	**transfer** Pure curd soap. **to 81.31 following** soaps have. **and read** That orangeflower water is so fresh.
525.1	82.16	**for** Pears' soap. **read** Pears' soap?
527.1	82.19	**for** Lyons' said. **read** Lyons said.
550.3	83.5	**for** mosque redbaked **read** mosque, redbaked
564.8	83.18–19	**for** dearer than them **read** dearer thaaan them

6: Hades

27.7	85.2	**for** number ten with **read** number nine with
48.5	85.22	**for** back, aying: **read** back, saying:
97.3	86.32	**for** this? he **read** this, he
122.6	87.19	**for** Doubles then up **read** Doubles them up
220.1	90.5	**delete dialogue dash, delete indent**
320.1	92.27	**for** Father Matew. Foundation **read** Father Mathew. Foundation
322.4–5	92.30	**for** A tinycoffin flashed **read** A tiny coffin flashed

329.13	92.36	**for** not the **read** not from the
355.1	93.24	**delete dialogue dash**
428.6	95.23	**for** up drowning **read** up, drowning
429.2	95.23–4	**for** A panse by **read** A pause by
453.3	96.9	**for** on. past **read** on past
498.10–499.1	97.14–15	**for** same, Pallbearers gold **read** same. Pallbearers, gold
522.7	98.1	**for** myself steping out **read** myself stepping out
559.6	99.1	**for** the, Cork **read** the Cork
576.1	99.18–19	**for** and the **read** and at the
607.5–6	100.13	**for** full of up bad **read** full up of bad
693.3	102.24	**for** said Madam **read** said, Madam
716.6	103.9	**for** two keys **read** two long keys
749.1	104.5	**for** death.. Shades **read** death. Shades
778.4	104.34	**for** earth lean. The **read** earth. The
853.4	106.34	**for** Bam! expires. **read** Bam! He expires.
871.6–7	107.14	**for** sure there'sns. **read** sure there's no.
929.3	108.34	**for** pillars family **read** pillars, family
965.5	109.31	**for** kraark awfullygladaseeragain hellohello **read** kraark awfullygladaseeagain hellohello
966.2–3	109.31–2	**for** hellohello amarawf kopthsth. Remind **read** hellohello amawf krpthsth. Remind

7: Aeolus

3.8	112.2	**for** trolley started **read** trolley, started
5.6–7, 6.1	112.4	**for** Sandymount, Green Rathmines, Ringsend, and **read** Sandymount Green, Rathmines, Ringsend and
18.3	112.16	**for** postcards, lettecards, parcels, **read** postcards, lettercards, parcels,
45.5	113.20	**for** passed stately up **read** passed statelily up
77.1–79.3	114.16–18	**transfer** WITH UNFEIGNED REGRET IT IS WE ANNOUNCE THE DISSOLUTION OF A MOST RESPECTED DUBLIN BURGESS **to 114.19–20 following** Thumping thump. **and begin 114.21** This morning **with a paragraph indent**
92.1	114.32	**for** of Tinnachinch. To **read** of Tinnahinch. To
97.4	115.5	**for** note M.A.P. **read** note. M.A.P.
123.6	115.30	**for** cutting a while and **read** cutting awhile and
128.7–13	115.32	**transfer** He doesn't hear it. Nannan. Iron nerves. **to 116.1 following** they make.
231.6–7	119.2	**for** see before dressing. **read** see: before: dressing.
245.7–10	119.14	**transfer** *fanned by gentlest zephyrs* **to 119.15 following** *mossy banks,* **and add comma after** *zephyrs*
244.3	119.14	**for** *tho' quarelling with* **read** *tho' quarrelling with*
321.9	121.21	**for** *regions for* **read** *regions, for*

326.1–3	121.24	**transfer** HIS NATIVE DORIC **to 121.25–6 following** forgot Hamlet.
329.7	121.28	**for** vent to to a **read** vent to a
450.8	125.17	**for** caricature cross the **read** caricature across the
494.8–9	126.26	**for** said: *Is it meet* **read** said: *It is meet*
496.7	126.27	**for** said, Our **read** said. Our
508.5	127.7	**for** suppliant, M. O'Madden **read** suppliant, Mr O'Madden
527.4	127.25	**for** mouth.? Are **read** mouth? Are
591.4	129.23	**for** *of Castille.* See **read** *of Castile.* See
604.1–2	130.1	**transfer** OMNIUM GATHERUM **to 130.2–3 following** Stephen said.
612.16–17	130.11	**for** coldin the **read** cold in the
623.5	130.21	**for** supply metanl pabulum, **read** supply mental pabulum,
638.12	131.4–5	**for** hat, Where **read** hat. Where
643.3	131.9	**for** know Holehan? **read** know Holohan?
685.3	132.15	**for** first. Thee was **read** first. There was
760.4–6	134.24	**for** J.J.O'Mollooy too kout his **read** J.J.O'Molloy took out his
762.5	134.26	**for** his match box **read** his matchbox
769.10	134.33	**for** *and prophecy* **read** *and of prophecy*
800.4–5	135.30	**for** sitting withim T Healy, **read** sitting with Tim Healy,
830.4	136.22	**for** *It senned to* **read** *It seemed to*

844.1	136.33	**for** good, could **read** good could
847.14	137.3	**for** *galleys, tireme and* **read** *galleys, trireme and*
903.4	138.24	**for** all night. **read** all right.
918.1	139.4	**for** – Yes, the **read** – Yes? the
926.2–4	139.12	**for** Off Blackpitts. **read** Off Blackpitts, Stephen said.
932.6–7	139.17	**for** and in tenpence a **read** and tenpence in a
962.1–3	140.12	**transfer** RETURN OF BLOOM **to 140.13–14 following** see them.
966.3	140.17	**for** Racing spécial! **read** Racing special!
998.10–999.1	141.16	**transfer** You must take the will for the deed. **to 141.17 following** Sorry, Jack.
1045.1–2	142.30–143.1	**for** Rathfarnham, Kingstown, Blackrock and **read** Rathfarnham, Blackrock, Kingstown and
1046.2–3	143.1–2	**for** Sandymount tower Donnybrook, **read** Sandymount Tower, Donnybrook,

8: Lestrygonians

21.1	144.21	**for** Phosphorous it **read** Phosphorus it
40.5–6	145.12–13	**for** reverence mum's **read** reverence. Mum's
79.5–9	146.15	**for** on fishy flesh they have to, all **read** on fish, fishy flesh they have, all
109.5	147.8	**for** one. Time ball on **read** one. Timeball on
116.14	147.14	**for** thinking, Still **read** thinking. Still
121.9	147.19	**for** at storing away **read** at stowing away

160.6	148.18	**for** dinner. Alterman Robert **read** dinner. Alderman Robert
164.9	148.22	**for** with selcovered buttons. **read** with selfcovered buttons.
168.7	148.25	**for** glove, shoulder and **read** glove, shoulders and
174.1	148.30	**for** papa's daguerrotype atelier **read** papa's daguerreotype atelier
239.5–6	150.18	**for** handbag chipped leather hatpin: **read** handbag, chipped leather, hatpin:
242.12	150.21	**for** Monday? Ave you **read** Monday? Are you
274.4	151.17	**for** Doyle's long' ago, **read** Doyle's long ago,
301.8	152.7	**for** question. Mrs **read** question? Mrs
343.9	153.12	**for** man, Weightcarrying **read** man. Weightcarrying
354.1	153.22	**for** *Express*. Scavening what **read** *Express*. Scavenging what
359.12–15	153.27	**for** dairy. Eating **read** dairy. Y.M.C.A. Eating
360.10–11	153.28	**for** minute. Still **read** minute. And still
364.12	153.32	**for** squallers Poor **read** squallers. Poor
425.7	155.16	**for** street. Luck I **read** street. Lucky I
425.11	155.16	**for** the presenee of **read** the presence of
455.2	156.8	**for** Ah, get along with **read** Ah, gelong with
459.13	156.12	**for** squad. Turkney's daughter **read** squad. Turnkey's daughter
500.1,5	157.14–15	**for** ware in Walter Sexton's window opposite by **read** ware opposite in Walter Sexton's window by

544.7	158.18	**for** be surpised if **read** be surprised if
594.6	159.32	**for** relief, his **read** relief his
600.6	160.1	**for** had, his **read** had his
609.2–3	160.9	**for** twentythree when **read** twentythree. When
615.2	160.14–15	**for** prints, silk, dames and **read** prints, silkdames and
691.4	162.11	**for** of news-paper. **read** of newspaper.
693.2	162.13	**for** Unchster Bunck un **read** Unchster Bunk un
737.2	163.18	**for** Bloom! Nosey **read** Bloom, Nosey
755.9	163.36	**for** itself. Mighty cheese. **read** itself. Mity cheese.
789.9	164.32	**for** mustard hauched on **read** mustard hanched on
867.14	166.33	**for** bed No. **read** bed. No.
892.10	167.20	**for** over first, finger **read** over fist, finger
903.1	167.30	**for** cities, Pillowed **read** cities. Pillowed
921.6	168.11	**for** Can seen them **read** Can see them
930.9	168.19–20	**for** stoking au engine. **read** stoking an engine.
1033.2	171.10	**broken** f **in** fully
1058.11–1059.10	172.2–3	**for** Presscott's ad. **read** Prescott's dyeworks van over there. If I got Billy Prescott's ad.
1067.4	172.9	**for** crusted kunckle. Handy **read** crusted knuckle. Handy
1096.7	173.1	**for** food I **read** food, I

1109.3–12	173.14	**for** Weight would **read** Weight or size of it, something blacker than the dark. Wonder would
1122.2–5	173.25–6	**for** together. Each **read** together. Each street different smell. Each

9: Scylla and Charybdis

52.3	177.25–6	**for** our mind into **read** our minds into
68.12	178.9	**for** of en ensouled **read** of an ensouled
108.5	179.13	**for** song, France **read** song. France
132.11	180.3	**for** one, Our **read** one. Our
179.2	181.15–16	**for** the dispossesed son: **read** the dispossessed son:
231.1	182.33	**second** f **in** softcreakfooted **broken**
232.12	182.35	**broken** f **in** of
235.5	183.1	**broken** f **in** from
240.9	183.6	**first** f **in** forgetfully **broken**
241.7	183.7	**broken** h **in** himself
243.11	183.9	**for** costard, guitless though **read** costard, guiltless though
250.1	183.16	**for** the bechamber of **read** the bedchamber of
340.9	185.33	**for** New place a **read** New Place a
426.1	188.3	**for** *d'être grand* ... **read** *d'être grandp* ...
456.13–457.1	188.27	**for** first (ryefield, **read** first (a ryefield,

492.5–6	189.24	**for** Photius, pseudomalachi, Johann **read** Photius, pseudo Malachi, Johann
541.6	191.3	**for** A shake coils **read** A snake coils
583.4	192.7	**for** *Master Silence* **read** *Master William Silence*
605.5	192.27	**for** Mulligan cried, **read** Mulligan cried.
610.2	192.32	**for** museum when I **read** museum where I
718.8	195.29–30	**for** bedsmiling, Let **read** bedsmiling. Let
757.6	196.32	**for** follow Sydney's. As **read** follow Sidney's. As
793.2	197.31	**for** Gentle will is **read** Gentle Will is
794.2	197.32	**for** will! gagged **read** will? gagged
832.7	198.34	**for** from Wittemberg then **read** from Wittenberg then
842.9	199.8	**for** unlikelihood, *Amor* **read** unlikelihood. *Amor*
851.10	199.16	**for** bestialities hardly **read** bestialities, hardly
870.8	199.34	**for** born for **read** born, for
939.4	202.3	**for** skies. *Autontimerumenos. Bous* **read** skies. *Autontimorumenos. Bous.*
940.11–12	202.4	**for** sua donna. **read** *sua donna.*
941.8	202.5	**for** *non amar S.D.* **read** *non amare S.D.*
959.3	202.23	**for** that marries **read** that always marries
1001.4	203.26–7	**for** *Two Gentleman of* **read** *Two Gentlemen of*
1014.7–8	204.3	**for** *Measure,* and **read** *Measure* – and

1028.6,11	204.16	**for** Dumas fils [...] Dumas père? **read** Dumas *fils* [...] Dumas *père?*
1043.9	204.30	**for** *doorstep, If* **read** *doorstep. If*
1059.7	205.10	**for** douce, herald, **read** douce herald,
1070.2	205.21	**for** John Eclection doubly **read** John Eclecticon doubly
1132.2	207.8	**for** the public sweat **read** the pubic sweat
1140.8	207.16	**for** forgot ... he ... **read** forgot ... eh ...
1161.2	208.4	**for** Yeats' touch? **read** Yeats touch?

10: Wandering Rocks

3.11	210.3	**for** was that that boy's **read** was that boy's
7.2	210.7	**for** A onlegged sailor, **read** A onelegged sailor,
15.8	210.15	**for** *I had served* **read** *I have served*
17.1	210.16	**for** leaves and **read** leaves: and
17.5	210.16–17	**for** him come the **read** him came the
27.15	211.2	**for** David Sheedy M.P. **read** David Sheehy M.P.
30.6–8	211.5	**for** hat, as **read** hat and smiled, as
40.3	211.15	**for** Conmee stropped three **read** Conmee stopped three
49.7	211.23	**for** and laughed. **read** and laughed:
100.9	212.33	**for** red, lying neatly **read** red, lie neatly
101.1	212.34	**no new paragraph at** Moored under

105.8	213.1	**for** bogs where men **read** bogs whence men
125.1	213.19	**new paragraph at** A tiny
139.5–8 139.14–140.1	213.32	bless you, my child, **and** pray for me. **in italic, not roman**
141.7	213.34	**for** Stratton grinned with **read** Stratton grimaced with
144.6	213.37	**for** sermon of Saint **read** sermon on Saint
172.3	214.27	**for** for men's race **read** for man's race
183.3–5	214.37	**for** homely and just **read** just and homely
197.1	215.12	**new paragraph with dialogue dash at** *Principium verborum*
201.3	215.16	**for** his hat abruptly: **read** his cap abruptly:
205.1	215.19	**new paragraph with dialogue dash at** *Principes persecuti*
239.12	216.16	**for** thanks and glanced **read** thanks, glanced
316.2	218.23–4	**for** hawker's car. **read** hawker's cart.
341.1	219.14–15	**for** gripping frankly the **read** gripping the
341.4	219.15	**for** handrests. Pale faces. Men's **read** handrests. Palefaces. Men's
345.14	219.19	**for** *bestia. E peccato.* **read** *bestia. È peccato.*
351.3	219.24	**for** *Ci refletta.* **read** *Ci rifletta.*
362.4	220.1	**for** Almidano Artifano said. **read** Almidano Artifoni said.
371.6	220.9	**for** it? Is **read** it. Is
383.2	220.20	**for** way she is holding **read** way she's holding

432.1	222.1	**for** His followed **read** He followed
445.15–16	222.15	**for** *didit, says* **read** *did it,* says
462.3	222.30	**for** was … this **read** was … Glasnevin this
523.3	224.17	**for** what he is buying, **read** what he's buying,
530.9	224.24	**for** about comet's tails **read** about comets' tails
604.9	226.20	**for** Listen: The **read** Listen: the
612.7	226.28	**for** *her deshabillé.* **read** *her deshabille.*
620.1	226.35–227.1	**for** yielded amid **read** yielded amply amid
623.2	227.3–4	**for** Press! Crished! Sulphur **read** Press! Chrished! Sulphur
645.3	227.26	**for** Dedalus, listening by **read** Dedalus, loitering by
658.11	228.5–6	**for** upon shoulders? Melancholy **read** upon shoulder? Melancholy
680.5	228.27	**for** five. Dilly **read** five, Dilly
698.7	229.8	**for** Look, that's all **read** Look, there's all
718.9	229.28	**for** Kernan pleased **read** Kernan, pleased
723.3	229.32–3	**for** weather we are having **read** weather we're having
731.2	230.5	**for** now you are talking **read** now you're talking
756.5	230.30	**for** Indian officier. Bravely **read** Indian officer. Bravely
757.11	230.31	**for** that Lambert's **read** that Ned Lambert's
767.1–768.3	231.2–3	**insert paragraph** Bad times those were. Well, well. Over and done with. Great topers too. Fourbottle men. **following** her noddy.

775.6	231.9	**for** outside ear without **read** outside car without
781.6	231.16	**no new paragraph at** Times of
819.10	232.17	**for** sanded umbrella, **read** sanded tired umbrella,
833.8	232.30	**for** in light loincloths **read** in tight loincloths
889.4	234.9	**for** Dedalus sald. Who **read** Dedalus said. Who
900.1	234.20	**for** – There he **read** – Here he
908.6	234.28	**for** to Fathes Cowley **read** to Father Cowley
919.4	235.4	**for** O'Connor Fitmaurice Tisdall **read** O'Connor Fitzmaurice Tisdall
984.2–4	236.32	*la Maison Claire* **in roman, not italic**
995.2	237.8	**for** And long John **read** And Long John
997.5	237.10	**for** of long John **read** of Long John
1015.10	237.26	**for** John Wise Nolan **read** John Wyse Nolan
1051.11	238.25	**no new paragraph at** An instant
1069.5	239.9	**for** forefinger. How I **read** forefinger. Now I
1099.1	240.1–2	**for** from Bridgewater with **read** from Bridgwater with
1102.6	240.5	**for** O'Connor Fiztmaurice Tisdall **read** O'Connor Fitzmaurice Tisdall
1109.6	240.12	**for** Wilde's he **read** Wilde's house he
1131.3	240.32	**for** him He **read** him. He
1173.2	242.1	**for** he is in **read** he's in

1182.8	242.10	**for** cordially greated on **read** cordially greeted on
1220.8	243.12	**for** charming *soubrette*, great **read** charming soubrette, great
1241.9	243.32	**for** in tanned shoes **read** in tan shoes
1242.13	243.34	**no new paragraph at** Blazes Boylan
1250.3	244.3	**for** the *cortège*: **read** the cortège:
1258.1	244.11	**delete paragraph indent**

11: Sirens

56.10	246.28	**for** ay, Like **read** ay. Like
96.2	247.32	**for** Your *beau,* is **read** Your beau, is
127.8–9	248.25	**for** for mercy'sake! **read** for mercy' sake!
145.2	249.5–6	**for** a shout in **read** a snout in
153.11–12	249.14	**for** with Dedalus'son. **read** with Dedalus' son.
230.12	251.12	**for** Blue Bloom is **read** Blue bloom is
267.11	252.11	**for** pundit. Hugh **read** pundit, Hugh
293.10	252.36	**for** to sees the **read** to see the
299.5	253.5	**for** mass. Tanks awfully **read** mass. Thanks awfully
343.9	254.9	**for** aloft saluting. **read** aloft, saluting.
390.5	255.18	**for** Goulding, Colles, Ward **read** Goulding, Collis, Ward
419.13–420.1	256.10–11	**for** tiny, chalice, **read** tiny chalice,
444.8	256.34	**for** orders, Power **read** orders. Power

452.6	257.5	**for** Plumped stopped **read** Plumped, stopped
486.8	258.1	**for** a yery trifling **read** a very trifling
500.2	258.15	**for** Mrs Marrion met **read** Mrs Marion met
520.11–12	258.35	**for** fried cods'roes while **read** fried cods' roes while
563.5	260.2	**for** Good afternoom. She **read** Good afternoon. She
575.3–4	260.11	**for** the'cello, **read** the cello,
580.4–5	260.16	**for** Lovely gold **read** Lovely. Gold
592.2	260.28	**for** headland wind **read** headland, wind
639.4	261.37	**for** moon Still **read** moon. Still
675.8	262.36	**for** strings of reeds **read** strings or reeds
687.2–3	263.11	**for** feet when **read** feet. When
701.5–6	263.25	**for** swelling, Full **read** swelling. Full
709.2	263.32–3	**for** joygush, tupthrop. Now! **read** joygush, tupthrob. Now!
722.2	264.9	**for** Drago's alway's looked **read** Drago's always looked
736.3	264.23	**for** all langour Lionel **read** all languor Lionel
740.1	264.27	**for** – *Co-me, thou* **read** – *Co-ome, thou*
741.1	264.28	**for** – *Co-me thou* **read** – *Co-ome thou*
766.6	265.18	**for** joggled tbe mare. **read** joggled the mare.
775.9	265.27	**for** in Lydia **read** in. Lydia
824.3	266.37	**for** Bloom, said, **read** Bloom said,
828.6	267.4	**for** opera. Goulding **read** opera, Goulding

840.13	267.16	**for** sacks over **read** sacks, over
844.10–846.5	267.19–21	**transfer** *Blumenlied* I bought for her. The name. Playing it slow, a girl, night I came home, the girl. Door of the stables near Cecilia street. **to the end of the paragraph following** I mean.
847.8	267.22	**for** ink Pat **read** ink. Pat
889.2	268.25	**for** know now. In **read** know how. In
889.10	268.25	**for** add postcript. What **read** add postscript. What
904.12	269.4–5	**for** charms Shakespeare **read** charms. Shakespeare
946.9	270.8	**for** sea. Corpuscule islands. **read** sea. Corpuscle islands.
952.9	270.14	**for** O', Böylan swayed **read** O', Boylan swayed
973.1–2	270.33	**for** silk. When **read** silk. Tongue when
1101.12 1102.12	274.11–12	**for** martyrs. For all things dying, want to, dying to, die. For that all things born. **read** martyrs that want to, dying to, die. For all things dying, for all things born.
1110.1	274.19	**new paragraph at** Ha. Lidwell.
1128.2	274.37	**for** music That **read** music. That
1143.10	275.12	**for** fat blackslapping, their **read** fat backslapping, their
1178.9	276.10	**for** left Bloom felt **read** left bloom felt
1257.10–12	278.12	**for** stroke. That appointment **read** stroke, that. Appointment
1263.2	278.17	**for** envisaged candlestick melodeon **read** envisaged candlesticks melodeon

12: Cyclops

8.11	280.8	**for** were taking to? **read** were talking to?
13.6	280.13	**for** There is a **read** There's a
19.1	280.18	**for** – Circumcised! says **read** – Circumcised? says
34.2–7	281.5	**for** parade, Wood **read** parade in the city of Dublin, Wood
38.9–11	281.8	**for** shillings per **read** shillings and no pence per
55.6	281.25	**for** he's in **read** he's out in
73.4–5	282.6	**for** flounder, the **read** flounder, the pollock, the
95.6	282.26	**for** and pumets of **read** and punnets of
101.2	282.31–2	**for** you notarious bloody **read** you notorious bloody
111.1	283.4	**for** of Lush and **read** of Lusk and
136.9	283.28	**for** rise, say he, **read** rise, says he,
174.5	284.27–8	**for** which dangled at **read** which jangled at
189.4	285.5	**for** Michelangelo, Hayes, **read** Michelangelo Hayes
210.7–8	285.24	**for** Joe? say I? **read** Joe? says I.
249.9	286.24	**for** door aud hid **read** door and hid
278.8	287.16	**for** Doran? Is **read** Doran. Is
281.5	287.19	**for** the foaming ebon **read** the foamy ebon
303.12	288.4–5	**for** hanging. I'll **read** hanging, I'll

304.8	288.5	**for** saw. Hangmens' letters. **read** saw. Hangmen's letters.
307.4	288.7	**for** codding? say I. **read** codding? says I.
331.4	288.31	**for** Alf. He is no **read** Alf. He's no
372.1	289.33	**no new paragraph at** Assurances were
398.3	290.22	**for** him to go **read** him go
399.10	290.23	**for** street that **read** street, that
409.8–11	290.33	**transfer** he won't eat you, **to the end of the line, and read** citizen. He won't eat you.
415.2	291.2	**insert dialogue dash**
436.2	291.21–2	**for** and couldn't **read** and he couldn't
441.1	291.27	**for** – There all **read** – They're all
471.6	292.21	**for** approved traditions of **read** approved tradition of
473.2–10	292.22–3	**for** centres, causing the pores **read** centres of the genital apparatus, thereby causing the elastic pores
478.1	292.26–7	**for** outwards philoprogenetive erection **read** outwards philoprogenitive erection
485.6	292.34	**for** brute sniffling and **read** brute sniffing and
486.7	292.35	**for** round be goes **read** round he goes
488.8	292.37	**for** with him: **read** with his:
489.12	293.1	**for the second** Give us the **read** Give the
495.11	293.7	**for** a Jacob's tin **read** a Jacobs' tin
561.3	294.33	**for** Hiram. Y. **read** Hiram Y.

565.9–566.3	294.37–295.1	**for** Goosepond Prhklstr Kratchinabritchisitch, Herr **read** Goosepond Přhklštř Kratchinabritchisitch, Borus Hupinkoff, Herr
612.4	296.6–7	**for** supplication. Hard by **read** supplication. Hand by
643.12	296.37	**for** would cherish **read** would ever cherish
660.10	297.16	**for** tree solicited **read** tree, solicited
663.13	297.18–19	**for** of skull **read** of a skull
668.10	297.23	**for** shamrock excitement **read** shamrock the excitement
701.8	298.18	**for** citizen, sneering. **read** citizen, jeering.
715.5–6	298.31	**for** red wolfdog setter formerly **read** red setter wolfdog formerly
729.6	299.7–8	**for** of Donald Mac **read** of Donal Mac
770.9	300.14	**for** about the mortgagor **read** about mortgagor
802.1	301.6	**for** bobby L, 14 A. **read** bobby, 14 A.
849.3	302.17	**for** egg, Ga **read** egg. Ga
888.7	303.19	**for** known. Do you **read** known. Did you
889.7	303.20	**for** Irish sport and **read** Irish sports and
889.13	303.20–21	**for** of the lawn **read** of lawn
902.1	303.32–3	**for** of this noble **read** of the noble
911.7	304.5	**for** and powers handed **read** and prowess handed
915.7	304.8	**for** house house, by **read** house, by
924.3	304.17	**for** audience amongst which **read** audience among which

932.1	304.24	**for** T.Maher. S.J. **read** T.Maher, S.J.
935.8–9	304.28	**for** C.C., the **read** C.C.; the
938.4–5	304.30	**for** C.C.; The **read** C.C. The
945.12	305.1–2	**for** training of the **read** training the
958.6	305.14	**for** wind. Queensberry **read** wind, Queensberry
994.3	306.11	**for** wife? say Bloom. **read** wife? says Bloom.
998.9	306.15	**for** the dodgers's son **read** the dodger's son
1002.10	306.19	**for** you Caddereesh. **read** you Caddareesh.
1029.12	307.8	**for** of these days, **read** of those days,
1045.3	307.23	**for** eye? says **read** eye! says
1060.10	307.37	**for** Bloom explained he **read** Bloom explaining he
1066.12	308.6	**for** The signor Brini **read** The signior Brini
1070.3	308.9	**for** with al kinds **read** with all kinds
1082.5	308.22	**for** went passed, talking **read** went past, talking
1107.2	309.10	**for** And a wife **read** And the wife
1117.5	309.20	**for** the claims of **read** the claim of
1157.2–3	310.22	**for** them. The **read** them in. The
1163.8	310.28	**for** citizen, that's what the **read** citizen, that was the
1194.8	311.22	**for** drawing un a **read** drawing up a
1203.1	311.31	**for** – There're not **read** – They're not
1251.6	313.3	**for** Cambrensis, Wine **read** Cambrensis. Wine

1259.8	313.11	**for** not to **read** not done to
1326.2	315.3	**for** up on a **read** up in a
1339.3	315.15	**for** called if but **read** called it but
1385.9	316.24	**for** masters? Do **read** masters! Do
1387.3–4	316.26	**for** an *Entente cordiale* now **read** an entente cordial now
1426.6	317.28	**for** had a laugh **read** had the laugh
1465.5	318.28	**for** drink? says **read** drink, says
1472.1	318.34–5	**for** auction off in **read** auction in
1490.12	319.16–17	**for** your neighbours. **read** your neighbour.
1506.11	319.33–4	**for** pocket What **read** pocket. What
1531.2–3	320.20	**for** executing an old **read** executing a charming old
1561.11	321.12	**for** round to the **read** round the
1574.7	321.24	**for** the idea for **read** the ideas for
1633.1–6	323.8	**transfer** – Who is Junius? says J.J. **to 323.6–7 as a separate paragraph following** offence, Crofton.
1721.8	325.19	**for** introit in *Epiphania* **read** introit *in Epiphania*
1725.7	325.23	**for** had beed mislaid, **read** had been mislaid,
1749.6	326.9	**for** *et animoe tutelam* **read** *et animae tutelam*
1754.5	326.13	**for** looking round to **read** looking around to
1756.7	326.15	**for** courthouse. says **read** courthouse, says
1789.15	327.11	**for** and be bawls **read** and he bawls

1807.2	327.29	**for** God! says **read** God? says
1822.5	328.6	**for** behalf on a **read** behalf of a
1840.13– 1841.4	328.24	**for** Pigeonhouse. *Visszontlátásra,* **read** Pigeonhouse, and the Poolbeg Light. *Visszontlátásra,*
1845.11	328.28	**for** play, in **read** play in
1848.4–5	328.30	**for** and J.G. paralysed **read** and J.J. paralysed
1873.9	329.18	**for** initials, coat **read** initials, crest, coat

13: Nausicaa

58.4	332.29–30	**for** troubles and and very **read** troubles and very
95.5	333.29	**for** not let **read** not to let
97.1–2	333.31	**for** There wasan innate **read** There was an innate
129.10	334.25	**for** a lover's quarrel **read** a lovers' quarrel
132.8	334.27–8	**for** him in the **read** him in in the
155.3–4	335.12	**for** the strideshowed off **read** the stride showed off
188.2–3	336.7	**for** yet and **read** yet – and
260.9,11	338.3	**for** about hin getting him own **read** about him getting his own
301.1	339.7	**for** was the **read** was that the
319.9	339.24–5	**for** so hear. Now **read** so near. Now
323.5	339.28	**for** artistic standard, **read** artistic, standard,

401.9	341.31	**for** always, readywitted, **read** always readywitted,
511.2–3	344.23	**for** shoulders, a **read** shoulders – a
513.15	344.26	**for** answering flush of **read** answering flash of
530.2	345.5	**for** their baby home **read** their babby home
579.6–7	346.15	**for** hurt. O **read** hurt – O
603.7–10	346.37	**for** them and **read** them and never would be and
611.12–15	347.9	**for** compliments on **read** compliments to all and sundry on
621.14	347.18	**for** put round him round **read** put round
639.1	347.34	**for** girlish treasures trove, **read** girlish treasure trove,
670.12	348.27	**for** follow her **read** follow, her
770.6–8	351.13	**for** because, because **read** because – because
776.8–9	351.19	**for** same. Wouldn't **read** same. I wouldn't
796.14	352.1	**for** her *deshabillé*. Excites **read** her *deshabille*. Excites
812.4	352.16	**for** cool coif and **read** cool coifs and
815.3	352.19	**for** comes, along **read** comes along
860.13–14	353.27	**for** behind coming **read** behind the wall coming
863.3	353.29	**for** however of you **read** however if you
864.10–865.2	353.31	**for** you're in **read** you're stuck. Gain time. But then you're in
1009.2	357.21	**for** No, Hyacinth? **read** No. Hyacinth?

1027.9	358.1	**broken** f **in last** of
1084.7	359.20	**for** worst, Friction **read** worst. Friction
1116.9	360.14	**for** the drew. **read** the dew.
1209.7	362.30	**for** *la muchaha hermosa.* **read** *la muchacha hermosa.*
1229.4	363.12	**for** was is outside **read** was it outside
1282.8–1283.6	364.26	**for** plump years **read** plump bubs me breadvan Winkle red slippers she rusty sleep wander years

14: Oxen of the Sun

5.7–8, 6.1	366.5–6	**for the third** Hoopsa, boyaboy hoopsa. **read** Hoopsa boyaboy hoopsa!
134.15	369.26	**for** and reproved the **read** and repreved the
140.6	369.31	**for** and sometimes venery. **read** and sometime venery.
157.6	370.10	**for** vast moutain. And **read** vast mountain. And
244.4	372.21	**for** as Virgillius saith, **read** as Virgilius saith,
306.3,5	374.6–7	**for** marriages *parce que M. Leo Taxil* **read** marriages *parceque M. Léo Taxil*
308.1	374.8	**for** *Entweder* transsubstantiality *oder* **read** *Entweder* transubstantiality *oder*
434.9	377.17	**for** Indeed not for **read** Indeed no for
441.8–13	377.23–4	**for** he and make **read** he though he must nor would he make

462.9	378.6	**for** these word printed **read** these words printed
532.6	379.36	**for** over to search **read** over the search
586.8–9	381.13	**for** of gold **read** of cloth of gold
631.8	382.18–19	**for** pulling it it out **read** pulling it out
634.10	382.21–2	**for** learn a a word **read** learn a word
637.8	382.24	**for** of rock **read** of a rock
672.1	383.19–20	**for** from proclivites acquired. **read** from proclivities acquired.
675.7	383.23	**for** in a uncongenial **read** in an uncongenial
708.1	384.16	**for** *ut matres familiarum nostrae* **read** *ut matresfamiliarum nostrae*
743.7	385.12	**for** polite breading had **read** polite breeding had
744.12	385.13	**for** the head asked **read** the bottle asked
767.2–3	385.34–5	**for** how greatand universal **read** how great and universal
791.8	386.20	**for** our heart and **read** our hearts and
846.9	387.36	**for** had born with **read** had borne with
851.10	388.4	**for** they scrupuluosly sensible **read** they scrupulously sensible
857.3	388.9	**for** his skill lent **read** his skull lent
878.1	388.29	**for** so ausspicated after **read** so auspicated after
906.13	389.19–20	**for** to civil rights, **read** to civic rights,
931.1	390.6	**for** an opprobium in **read** an opprobrium in

963.7	390.36	**for** the agnatia of **read** the agnathia of
967.1	391.3	**for** the prolungation of **read** the prolongation of
971.8	391.7	**for** the perpetration of **read** the perpetuation of
974.5	391.10	**for** and monstruous births **read** and monstrous births
1029.7	392.25–6	**for** of Mannanaun! The **read** of Mananaun! The
1047.1	393.5	**for** in Clambrassil street **read** in Clanbrassil street
1061.6	393.18–19	**for** shrivels, to **read** shrivels, dwindles to
1075.10–11	393.32	**for** thee and **read** thee – and
1148.9	395.28	**for** that Periplepomenos sells **read** that Periplepomenes sells
1153.1	395.32	**for** that it is, **read** that she is,
1178.8	396.19	**for** to exibit symptoms **read** to exhibit symptoms
1192.10	396.32–3	**for** he involontarily determined **read** he involuntarily determined
1196.1	396.36	**for** time however, however, **read** time, however,
1212.8	397.14–15	**for** elegance and and townbred **read** elegance and townbred
1216.11	397.18	**for** were accomodated the **read** were accommodated the
1229.9	397.30	**for** some questons which **read** some questions which

1248.5	398.11	**for** the suspened carcases **read** the suspended carcases
1289.5	399.13	**for** cancrenous femoules emaciated **read** cancrenous females emaciated
1375.9	401.21	**for** of danger *read* of the danger
1378.3	401.24	**for** (*alles vergängliche*) in **read** (*alles Vergängliche*) in
1405.9	402.14	**for** when come the **read** when comes the
1430.3–4	402.37	**for** never do. read never – do.
1450.1	403.19	**for** gun. Burke's! Thence **read** gun. Burke's! Burke's! Thence
1450.9–1451.1	403.20	**for** foot where's **read** foot. Where's
1482.5	404.13	**for** gert wool. Well, **read** gert vool. Well,
1500.7	404.31	**for** acoming, Underconstumble? **read** acoming. Underconstumble?
1532.7	405.25	**for** mon, wee **read** mon, a wee
1539.5,7	405.31	**for** Kristyann will yu help, yung **read** Kristyann wil yu help yung
1540.9	405.32	**for** crown off his **read** crown of his
1546.4	406.1	**for** tunket's you guy **read** tunket's yon guy
1554.1	406.8	**for** Pardon? See him **read** Pardon? Seen him
1555.3	406.9	**for** Pore piccanninies! Thou'll **read** Pore piccaninnies! Thou'll
1569.7	406.23	**for** Pflaap! Blase on. **read** Pflaap! Blaze on.
1584.7–9	406.37	**for** Dowie, that's **read** Dowie, that's my name, that's

1587.4	407.3	**for** business propostion. He's **read** business proposition. He's

15: Circe

3.7	408.3	**for** *of flimsy houses* **read** *of grimy houses*
6.10	408.6	**for** *of coal and* **read** *of coral and*
20.10	408.19	**for** *gurgles.)* Grhahute! **read** *gurgles.)* Ghahute!
26.3	409.4	**for** *between the railings,* **read** *between two railings,*
27.9	409.5	**for** *hat moves, groans,* **read** *hat snores, groans,*
30.8	409.8	**for** *rams the last* **read** *rams her last*
41.6	409.18	**for** *a scrufulous child.* **read** *a scrofulous child.*
78.9	410.23	**for** *bawd protude from* **read** *bawd protrude from*
81.8	410.25	**for** Come, here **read** Come here
98.5	411.14	**for** *Salvi facti i sunt.* **read** *Salvi facti sunt.*
105.11	411.21	**for** not odours, would **read** not odour, would
117.9	412.5	**for** bread and wine **read** bread or wine
151.1	413.6–7	**for** *bright arclamps. He* **read** *bright arclamp. He*
155.5	413.10	**for** *into Olhousen's, the* **read** *into Olhausen's, the*
161.3	413.15	**for** *his rib and* **read** *his ribs and*
178.8	414.3	**for** *lanterns awsing, swim* **read** *lanterns aswing, swim*

195.7–8	414.20	**for** the hattrick? **read** the hat trick?
198.1	414.21	**transfer** BLOOM **to 414.23–4 as a speech heading following** *parcelled hand.)*
200.2	414.25	**for** Sandow's exerciser again. **read** Sandow's exercises again.
202.7	414.27	**for** in tracks or **read** in track or
202.13	414.27	**for** Day, the **read** Day the
206.13	415.2	**for** all he same. **read** all the same.
226.1–228.2	415.20	**following** I beg. **insert indented narrative direction** (*He leaps right, sackragman right.*) **plus speech heading** BLOOM **plus speech** I beg.
231.11	415.23	**for** a fingerpost planted **read** a signpost planted
233.13	415.25–6	**for** *In darkset Stepaside.* **read** *In darkest Stepaside.*
242.8–243.1	416.4	**for** *hands watch, fobpocket, bookpocket, pursepoke,* **read** *hands watchfob, pocketbookpocket, pursepoke,*
243.6	416.5	**for** *sin, potato soap.)* **read** *sin, potatosoap.)*
245.5	416.7	**for** Old thieves dodge. **read** Old thieves' dodge.
247.4–5	416.9	**for** *retriever approches sniffling, nose* **read** *retriever approaches, sniffing, nose*
275.1	417.7–8	**for** you kaput, Leopoldleben. **read** you kaputt, Leopoldleben.
283.7–8	417.16	**place** *Widow Twankey's* **between** *mobcap,* **and** *crinoline*
285.4–5	417.18	**for** *her hair plaited in* **read** *her plaited hair in*

311.10	418.12	**for** *her, excuses, desire,* **read** *her, excuse, desire,*
319.2	418.20	**for** Nebrakada! Feminimum! **read** Nebrakada! Femininum!
353.1–7	419.21	**transfer** *plump as a pampered pouter pigeon* **to the end of the narrative direction and read** Giovanni, *plump* [...] *pigeon.*)
386.3	420.29	**for** (*She slides away* **read** (*She glides away*
398.13	421.11	**for** think me? **read** think of me?
399.6	421.12	**for** have hears. How **read** Have ears. How
445.4	422.27	**for** thoughtreading! Subject, **read** thoughtreading? Subject,
445.10	422.27	**for** this snuffbox! **read** this snuffbox?
450.8–10	423.2	**for** *with watered silkfacings, blue* **read** *with wateredsilk facings, blue*
451.8	423.3	**for** *mother-of-pear studs,* **read** *mother-of-pearl studs,*
480.1	423.29	**for** *Hely's sandwichboard, shuffles* **read** *Hely's sandwichboards, shuffles*
482.7	424.2	**for** *spades dogs* **read** *spades, dogs*
488.9	424.7	**for** well! You **read** well? You
496.8	424.15	**for** Mrs Bandman Palmer. **read** Mrs Bandmann Palmer.
498.5	424.17	**for** for pig's feet. **read** for pigs' feet.
559.2	426.20	**for** cruel creature, **read** cruel naughty creature,
600.1–603.9	428.2–5	**delete inset and read as four speeches**
603.3	428.5	**for** come her till **read** come here till

633.4	429.8	**for** *dog approches, his* **read** *dog approaches, his*
653.3	429.28	**for** *the sicksewet weed* **read** *the sicksweet weed*
658.10	430.1	**for** and eight pence too **read** and eightpence too
662.7	430.5	**for** mad. Fido. Uncertain **read** mad. Dogdays. Uncertain
662.12–663.1–2	430.5	**for** movements. Good **read** movements. Good fellow! Fido! Good
672.6	430.13	**for** *lets unrolled* **read** *lets the unrolled*
703.9	431.13	**for** *with diamonds studs* **read** *with diamond studs*
706.3	431.16	**for** *boarhound.* **read** *boarhound.)*
711.2	431.21	**for** strangling pully will **read** strangling pulley will
721.13	431.31–2	**for** von Bloom Pasha. **read** von Blum Pasha.
753.10	432.30	**for** Henry! Leopold! Leopold! Lionel, **read** Henry! Leopold! Lionel,
762.9	433.8	**for** hatchet, I **read** hatchet. I
770.3	433.16	**for** *the past of* **read** *the pass of*
812.5	434.26	**for** *Weekly Arsewiper* here. **read** *Weekly Arsewipe* here.
823.3	435.5	**for** a literateur. It's **read** a *littérateur*. It's
824.8	435.7	**for** bestselling books, really **read** bestselling copy, really
836.4	435.19	**for** we! We **read** we? We
843.11	435.26	**for** evidence the **read** evidence, the

875.5	436.27	**for** *ripplecloth flannel* **read** *ripplecloth, flannel*
876.3	436.28	**for** *rumpled softly.)* **read** *rumpled: softly.)*
895.1	437.19	**for** GEORGES FOTTRELL **read** GEORGE FOTTRELL
901.4	437.24–5	**for** *but, through branded* **read** *but, though branded*
904.1	437.27	**for** *A seven months child* **read** *A sevenmonths' child*
916.7–8	438.8	**for** *pensums, model* **read** *pensums or model*
928.9	438.19–20	**outset** (*From the* […] *and calls.*) **as a speech direction, and run on** Cough it […] in bits.)
952.4–5	439.10	**for** unfold one **read** unfold – one
971.6	439.29	**for** accused, was **read** accused was
986.3	440.9	**for** (*The mirage of* **read** (*The image of*
987.5	440.10	**for** *projected ou the* **read** *projected on the*
996.8	440.19	**for** *rosepink blood.* **read** *rosepink blood.)*
1005.1–2	440.26–7	**position** (*A paper* […] *into court.*) **as a separate narrative direction**
1031.10	441.19	**for** and ballstop **read** and the ballstop
1048.3	442.2–3	**for** and ffeecy sheepskins **read** and fleecy sheepskins
1054.4–5,16	442.8–9	**enclose** stating that […] urge me **in parentheses, not commas**
1081.10	443.2	**for** *of sudden fury.)* **read** *of fury.)*
1092.2	443.13	**for** MRS YELUERTON BARRY **read** MRS YELVERTON BARRY
1107.6	443.28	**for** *hands with* **read** *hands: with*

1173.1–2,9	446.2–3	**transfer** (*A black* [...] *his head.*) **to the beginning of the following narrative direction, and delete the redundant parentheses**
1189.4	446.19	**for** Lewd chimpanzees. (*Breathlessly.*) **read** Lewd chimpanzee. (*Breathlessly.*)
1204.4	447.5	**for** *beagle lift his* **read** *beagle lifts his*
1210.10	447.11	**for** true. it was **read** true. It was
1241.11	448.13	**for** Jacobs Vobiscuits. **read** Jacobs. Vobiscuits.
1246.12–13	448.17	**for** *forward, places* **read** *forward and places*
1267.5–1268.9	449.6	**for** *again. He* **read** *again through the sump. Kisses chirp amid the rifts of fog. A piano sounds. He*
1273.3	449.11	**for** coocoo! Yummyumm Womwom! **read** coocoo! Yummyyum, Womwom!
1296.11	450.5	**for** *hand slides over* **read** *hand glides over*
1332.1–2–1333.8	451.11–13	**treat** (*Murmuring singsong* [...] *and rosewater.*) **as a speech direction, and run on** *Schorach ani* [...] *benoith Hierushaloim.*
1383.2	453.3	**for** alderman, sir **read** alderman sir
1399.2	453.19	**for** *up A* **read** *up. A*
1411.6	453.30	**for** *civic flåg. The* **read** *civic flag. The*
1415.3–4	453.33	**for** *Dublin, the* **read** *Dublin, his lordship the*
1431.3	454.14–15	**for** *manufacturers, understakers, silk* **read** *manufacturers, undertakers, silk*
1529.12	457.13	**for** *uttering thier warcry,* **read** *uttering their warcry,*
1559.4	458.13	**for** *elongated figure at* **read** *elongated finger at*

1565.9	458.19	**for** *macintosh disppears. Bloom* **read** *macintosh disappears. Bloom*
1576.8	458.29–30	**for** *and prvileged Hungarian* **read** *and privileged Hungarian*
1583.8	459.3	**for** *Reached 'Our Heart* **read** *Reached Our Heart*
1591.4	459.11	**for** Little Father **read** Little Father!
1601.15	459.20	**for** (*He playes pussy* **read** (*He plays pussy*
1605.2	459.23	**for** *silk haudkerchiefs from* **read** *silk handkerchiefs from*
1619.3	460.4	**for** (*The ram's horns* **read** (*The rams' horns*
1652.2	461.5	**for** *Tinct. mix. vom,* **read** *Tinct. nux. vom.,*
1653.3	461.6	**for** *taraxel. lig. 30* **read** *taraxel. liq., 30*
1691.6–8	462.17	**for** the universal **read** the universal language with universal
1693.3–4	462.18	**for** money, free **read** money, free rent, free
1731.13	463.26	**for** of Casteele **read** of Casteele.
1732.1–3	463.27	**position** (*Laughter.*) **as a separate narrative direction**
1766.4–5	464.29–30	**for** *bread, sheeps'tails, odd* **read** *bread, sheeps' tails, odd*
1771.5–7	465.5	**for** *sgenl inn ban* **read** *sgeul im barr*
1803.1	466.3–4	**for** Reformed Priests Protection **read** Reformed Priests' Protection
1805.12–1806.2	466.6	**for** hairshirt winter **read** hairshirt of pure Irish manufacture winter
1823.4–5	466.24	**for** *All are* **read** *All the octuplets are*

1838.4–7	467.4	**for** a miracle. **read** a miracle like Father Charles.
1853.1–2	467.18–20	**reposition** (*In papal* [...] *paper mitre.*) **as a speech direction, and run on** *Leopoldi autem*
1893.4	468.22	**for** see kay **read** see Kay
1905.1	469.5–6	**for** *earlocks, They* **read** *earlocks. They*
1907.9	469.8	**for** Messiah! Abulafia! **read** Messiah! Abulafia! Recant!
1936.11–12	470.4–6	**reposition** (*He exhibits* [...] *of burning.*) **as a speech direction running on from** of Erin. **and position** (*The daughters* [...] *and pray.*) **as a separate narrative direction**
1953.10	470.20	**for** *by Mr Vincent* **read** *by Vincent*
1954.3–1955.2	470.21	**for** *the Alleluia chorus, accompanied* **read** *the chorus from Handel's Messiah* Alleluia for the Lord God omnipotent reigneth, *accompanied*
1960.11	470.26	**for** *band, dsuty brogues,* **read** *band, dusty brogues,*
1974.15–1975.4	471.6	**for** and bottle. **read** and bottle. I'm sick of it. Let everything rip.
1980.7	471.11	**for** very disagreable. You **read** very disagreeable. You
2033.7	473.2	**for** *waterproof, Bloom* **read** *waterproof. Bloom*
2035.3	473.3	**for** *is thrown open.* **read** *is flung open.*
2035.12	473.4	**for** *trousers brownsocked,* **read** *trousers, brownsocked,*
2053.10	473.21	**for** *the mantlepiece. A* **read** *the mantelpiece. A*
2058.14	473.26	**for** *with the wand.* **read** *with his wand.*

2111.12	475.13	**for** possible elipse. Consistent **read** possible ellipse. Consistent
2151.6	476.22	**for** *hydrocephalic, prognatic with* **read** *hydrocephalic, prognathic with*
2166.5	477.7	**for** *torpor, crosses herself* **read** *torpor, crossing herself*
2183.4	477.24	**for** *the passing drift* **read** *the possing drift*
2189.13	477.29–30	**for** Sue, Dave Campbell, **read** Sue, Dove Campbell,
2211.6	478.18–20	**position** (*Drowning his voice.*) **as a speech direction, and run on** Whorusalaminyourhighhohhhh ... (*The disc* [...] *the needle.*)
2227.8–2228.1	479.1	**for** bishop. My **read** bishop and enrolled in the brown scapular. My
2234.1	479.6–7	**for** three stars. I **read** three star. I
2247.8	479.20	**for** *in hairdresser attire,* **read** *in hairdresser's attire,*
2262.6	480.4	**for** *of Mananann Mac* **read** *of Mananaun Mac*
2263.12	480.5	**for** *druid mantle. About* **read** *druid mouth. About*
2267.1	480.9	**for** MHANANANN MAC **read** MANANAUN MAC
2280.2	480.21	**for** Pooah! Pfuiiiiii! **read** Pooah! Pfuiiiiiii!
2333.11	482.6	**for** today Parallax! **read** today. Parallax!
2350.7	482.22	**for** brands mlld, medium **read** brands mild, medium
2351.5	482.23	**for** happy caould you **read** happy could you

2373.3	483.12	**for** and Ichthyosaurus. For **read** and Ichthyosauros. For
2400.12	484.5	**for** of 1882 to **read** of 1886 to
2405.4	484.9	**for** *surveys incertainly the* **read** *surveys uncertainly the*
2410.1	484.13–14	**for** then tomorrow as **read** then morrow as
2412.2	484.16	**for** (*Prompts into his ear in* **read** (*Prompts in*
2414.5	484.18	**for** pudendal verve in **read** pudendal nerve in
2427.3–9	484.30	**for** Charley! Buzz! **read** Charley! (*He blows in Bloom's ear.*) Buzz!
2433.11	485.3	**for** (*He gabbles gluttonously* **read** (*He gobbles gluttonously*
2442.6–10	485.11	**for** my ocular. **read** my ocular. (*He sneezes.*) Amen!
2446.2	485.15	**for** serpent contradict. Not **read** serpent contradicts. Not
2453.6	485.22	**for** been the known … **read** been the the known …
2462.1–2	485.30	**for** Who's Ger Ger? Who's **read** Who's moth moth? Who's
2462.6–14	485.31	**for** Gerald? O, **read** Gerald? Dear Ger, that you? O dear, he is Gerald. O,
2465.6	485.33	**for** *mews.*) Luss puss **read** *mews.*) Puss puss
2467.2–11	485.34	**for** rest anon. **read** rest anon. (*He snaps his jaws suddenly in the air.*)
2477.1–7	486.9–10	**position** Pretty pretty […] pretty petticoats. **as a separate line, inset**
2478.8	486.11	**for** *two sliding steps* **read** *two gliding steps*

49

2573.7,9	489.9	**for** Judas Iacchias, a Lybian eunuch, **read** Judas Iacchia, a Libyan eunuch,
2580.11	489.15	**for** all suscribed for **read** all subscribed for
2598.2	490.4	**for** (*Agueschaken, profuse* **read** (*Agueshaken, profuse*
2614.7–8	490.19	**for** Ben Mac Chree! **read** Ben my Chree!
2621.5	490.26	**for** (*He pluks his* **read** (*He plucks his*
2649.7	491.25	**for** sure you are a **read** sure you're a
2672.1	492.20	**for** Hi-hi-hi-hi-his legs **read** Hihihihihis legs
2677.7	492.25	**for** *swarms over* **read** *swarms white over*
2702.7	493.17	**for** *briskly.*) Hum. Thank **read** *briskly.*) Hmmm! Thank
2713.7	493.27–8	**run on** Catch. **to follow** *eyes her.*)
2734.5	494.18	**for** *heelclacking is* **read** *heelclacking tread is*
2736.7–9	494.20	**for** Aphrodisiac? But **read** Aphrodisiac? Tansy and pennyroyal. But
2751.4	495.3	**for** *glances around her* **read** *glances round her*
2764.7	495.15	**for** *her eardrop.*) **read** *her left eardrop.*)
2769.15	495.20	**for** now we? **read** now me?
2814.10	497.8	**for** in Mansfield's was **read** in Manfield's was
2816.9	497.10	**for** incredibly small, **read** incredibly impossibly small,
2827.2	497.21	**for** luck. Nook in **read** luck. Hook in
2845.6	498.8	**for** *semiflexed.*) Magnificence! **read** *semiflexed.*) Magmagnificence!

2851.10–11	498.13	**for** *closing.*) Truffles! **read** *closing, yaps.*) Truffles!
2857.10	498.19	**for** *rings ronnd his* **read** *rings round his*
2860.13	498.22	**for** *in.*) Feel **read** *in.*) Footstool! Feel
2882.6	499.11	**for** dear. I **read** dear, I
2901.10–11	499.29–30	**run on** (*He twists* [...] *turning turtle.*) **as a speech direction following** hurt you.
2902.1	499.30	**for** *Bloom squeaks, turning* **read** *Bloom squeals, turning*
2929.1–2	500.24–5	**reposition** (*They hold and pinion Bloom.*) **as a separate narrative direction**
2931.2	500.26	**for** (*Squats, with* **read** (*Squats with*
2932.12	500.27	**for** elected chairman of **read** elected vicechairman of
2934.8	500.29	**for** that I didn't **read** that didn't
2953.6	501.17	**for** Me Me. **read** Me. Me.
2959.1	501.22–3	**for** *farts loudly.*) Take **read** *farts stoutly.*) Take
2985.2	502.16	**for** (*A charming soubrette* **read** (*Charming soubrette*
2986.13	502.17	**for** only once, a **read** only twice, a
3003.8	503.2	**for** liftboy, Henry Fleury **read** liftboy, Henri Fleury
3025.4	503.23	**for** the Dorans' you'll **read** the Dorans you'll
3032.6	503.30	**for** he encouraged **read** he frankly encouraged
3045.1	504.8	**for** *Booloohoom. Poldy* **read** *Booloohoom, Poldy*
3045.6	504.8	**for** *penny. Cassidy's* **read** *penny, Cassidy's*

3047.1–4	504.10	**for** *other, the …)* **read** *other the, lane the.*)
3055.8	504.18	**for** Two! Thr … ! **read** Two! Thr …
3067.7	504.30	**for** tail, Won't **read** tail. Won't
3068.15– 3069.1	504.31	**for** Say, thank you mistress. **read** Say, *thank you mistress.*
3095.1–3096.1	505.26–7	**transfer** THE LACQUEY Barang! **to 503.23–4 following** *his handbell.*)
3099.3	505.28	**for** ALBERTA MARSH. **read** ALBERTA MARSH
3119.11	506.14	**for** Louis XV heels, **read** Louis Quinze heels,
3121.5	506.16	**for** your power of **read** your powers of
3131.2	506.24	**for** limp a **read** limp as a
3158.2–3,5	507.19	**for** Rip Van Winkle! Rip Van Winkle! **read** Rip van Wink! Rip van Winkle!
3164.1	507.25	**for** BELLA **read** BELLO
3176.5–6	508.5	**for** you, say? Following **read** you, eh, following
3176.10	508.5	**for** streets,, flatfoot **read** streets, flatfoot
3202.8–9	508.28–9	**reposition** (*He bites his thumb.*) **as a speech direction running on from** Has nobody … ?
3212.13	509.8	**for** Byby. Papli! **read** Byby, Papli!
3215.15–16	509.10–11	**reposition** (*He weeps tearlessly.*) **as a speech direction running on from** have suff …
3223.8	509.18	**for** *Watchman, O.Mastiansky,* **read** *Watchman, P.Mastiansky,*
3224.5	509.19	**for** *Abramovitz, Chazen. With* **read** *Abramovitz, chazen. With*

3227.2	509.22	**for** (*In a dark* **read** (*In dark*
3242.7	510.4	**for** *the bought, streaked* **read** *the bough, streaked*
3249.12–13	510.11	**for** youth, adsf or transparencies, **read** youth, ads for transparencies,
3273.10	511.3	**for** of my bed **read** of bed
3285.7	511.15	**for** *her hand.*) What **read** *her hands.*) What
3310.1–3314.1	512.6–7	**following** our shade? **insert** BLOOM (*Scared.*) High School of Poula? Mnemo? Not in full possession of faculties. Concussion. Run over by tram. THE ECHO Sham!
3319.1	512.10	**for** my tens, a **read** my teens, a
3321.4–5, 3322.4–5	512.12,13–14	**enclose** for they love [...] unbridles vice **in parentheses, and read** stairs (for [...] vice), even
3333.5	512.23	**for** *mammamufflered, stunned with* **read** *mammamufflered, starred with*
3353.6	513.11	**for** The fauns. I **read** The fauna. I
3356.3	513.14	**for** toilette trough illclosed **read** toilette through illclosed
3358.13	513.16	**for** and I ... A **read** and I. A
3360.5	513.18	**for** a white polled calf, **read** a whitepolled calf,
3363.1–10	513.21	**add initial speech direction** (*Large teardrops rolling from his prominent eyes, snivels.*)
3365.5	513.23	**for** need. (*With* **read** need I ... (*With*

3370.4	513.28	**for** (*Bleats.*) Megegaggegg! Nannannanny! **read** (*Bleats.*) Megeggaggegg! Nannannanny!
3372.10	513.30	**for** *and gorsepine.*) Regularly **read** *and gorsespine.*) Regularly
3377.1–2	514.3–5	**reposition** (*Through silversilent* [...] *waiting waters.*) **as a separate narrative direction**
3381.1	514.7	**for** Bbbbbllllbbbbblblobschbg! **read** Bbbbbllllblblblblobschb!
3386.13	514.12–13	**for** *waistcoat, opening,* **read** *waistcoat opening,*
3397.2	514.23	**for** (*Pacing the* **read** (*Pawing the*
3418.2	515.13	**for** (*From the* **read** (*In the*
3439.7	516.4	**for** *backtrousers' button snaps.*) **read** *back trouserbutton snaps.*)
3456.1–12	516.21	**precede** Sacrilege! To **with a new speech direction** (*Her features hardening, gropes in the folds of her habit.*)
3459.2	516.23	**for** *clutches in* **read** *clutches again in*
3463.11	516.27	**for** Cat of nine **read** Cat o' nine
3464.13	516.28–9	**for** do we lack **read** do you lack
3477.3	517.10	**for** alimony to morrow, eh? **read** alimony tomorrow, eh?
3477.14	517.10–11	**for** *sniffs.*) But, Onions. **read** *sniffs.*) Rut. Onions.
3484.3	517.17	**for** and superflous hair. **read** and superfluous hair.
3490.1	517.22	**for** *barks.*) Fohracht! **read** *barks.*) Fbracht!
3492.10–3493.1	517.24–5	**for** first, the cold spunk of your bully is **read** first, your bully's cold spunk is

3513.7–9	518.16	**for** nothing but still a **read** nothing, but still, a
3533.3	519.7	**for** (*With exagerated politeness.*) **read** (*With exaggerated politeness.*)
3542.6–8	519.16	**for** *money, then* **read** *money, then at Stephen, then*
3542.12	519.16	**for** *Zoe, Florrie and* **read** *Zoe, Florry and*
3549.3	519.23	**for** *in monosyllabbes. Zoe* **read** *in monosyllables. Zoe*
3549.5–6	519.23	**for** *Zoe bounds over to the* **read** *Zoe bends over the*
3550.2	519.24	**for** *neck, Lynch* **read** *neck. Lynch*
3588.4	521.2	**for** (*Points.*) Hum? Deep **read** (*Points.*) Him? Deep
3589.1–2	521.2–3	**reposition** (*Lynch bends* [...] *to Stephen.*) **as a separate narrative direction**
3621.5	522.4	**for** *table Stephen* **read** *table. Stephen*
3628.5	522.10	**for** *match nearer his* **read** *match near his*
3642.3,5	522.24	**for** *it into the gate.*) **read** *it in the grate.*)
3653.4	523.6	**for** alle kaput. **read** alle kaputt.
3668.3	523.20	**for** *bald tittle round* **read** *bald little round*
3673.11	523.24	**for** *John Connee rises* **read** *John Conmee rises*
3675.3	523.26	**for** JOHN CONNEE **read** JOHN CONMEE
3710.5–6	525.2–3	**run on** (*She sidles* [...] *waddles off.*) **as a speech direction following** Klook. Klook.
3714.3	525.6	**for** years age. I **read** years ago. I
3718.9–3719.2	525.10	**for** twentytwo too. **read** twentytwo. Sixteen years ago he was twentytwo too.

3737.6–8	525.27–8	**for** (*They whisper again.*) **read** (*She whispers again.*) **and run on as a speech direction following** *Florry.*) Whisper.
3738.13	525.29	**for** *straw, set* **read** *straw set*
3739.9	525.30	**for** *in a yachtsman's* **read** *in yachtsman's*
3741.2	526.1–2	**for** *Boylan's shoulder.*) **read** *Boylan's coat shoulder.*)
3758.3	526.19	**for** Bloom up yet? **read** Bloom dressed yet?
3760.2,4	526.21	**for** (*In a flunkey's plum plush* **read** (*In flunkey's prune plush*
3764.8	526.25	**for** *Bloom's autlered head.*) **read** *Bloom's antlered head.*)
3782.1–3784.5	527.13–14	**insert** BOYLAN (*Clasps himself.*) Here, I can't hold this little lot much longer. (*He strides off on stiff cavalry legs.*)
3792.8	527.21	**for** *holds an* **read** *holds out an*
3809.12–3810.1	528.8–9	**for** Ah! Gooblazeqruk brukarchkrasht! **read** Ah! Godblazegrukbrukarchkhrasht!
3812.10–3813.1	528.11–12	**for** Weeshwashtkissimapooisthnapoohuck! **read** Weeshwashtkissinapooisthnapoohuck!
3829.1	528.26–7	**for** his Thursdaymomun. Iagogogo! **read** his Thursdaymornun. Iagogogo!
3831.6	528.29	**for** *the whores.*) **read** *the three whores.*)
3836.2	529.5	**for** taken near the **read** taken next the
3838.3	529.7	**for** *deathtalk, fears and* **read** *deathtalk, tears and*
3840.2	529.8	**for** *nose a* **read** *nose, a*

3842.7,11	529.11	**for** *Scottish widow's insurance policy and large* **read** *Scottish Widows' insurance policy and a large*
3843.8	529.12	**for** *brood runs with* **read** *brood run with*
3844.11	529.12	**for** *one short foot,* **read** *one shod foot,*
3845.8	529.14	**for** *crying cods' mouth,* **read** *crying cod's mouth*
3858.4	529.25	**for** *bowing, twisting japanesily.)* **read** *bowing, twirling japanesily.)*
3880.10	530.16	**for** Rmm Rrrrrrmmmmm. **read** Rmm Rrrrrrmmmm.
3883.1	530.18–19	**for** to expenses your **read** to expense your
3884.2	530.19–20	**for** perhaps her heart **read** perhaps hers heart
3894.1–2	530.29	**for** *Ho, la la! Ce* **read** *Ho, là là! Ce*
3900.1,9	531.4	**for** *(Grimacing with […] clapping himself.)* **read** *(With head back, laughs loudly, clapping himself grimacing.)*
3906.4–5	531.9	**for** lifesize tompeeptoms virgins **read** lifesize tompeeptom of virgins
3907.8	531.10–11	**for** in mirrors every **read** in mirror every
3909.7	531.12	**for** or omlette on **read** or omlet on
3928.2	532.2	**for** Dreams go by **read** Dreams goes by
3930.2	532.4	**for** *(Extending his* **read** *(Extends his*
3941.3	532.15	**for** *sharpened.)* Hola! Hillyho! **read** *sharpened.) Holà!* Hillyho!
3946.3	532.19	**for** *of hearkening, on* **read** *of heartening, on*
3950.9	532.23	**for** Bulbul! Burblblbrurblbl! Hai, **read** Bulbul! Burblblburblbl! Hai,

3951.11	532.24	**for** *rapidly across country. A* **read** *rapidly crosscountry. A*
3953.3,6	532.26	**for** *swift, for the open brighteyed,* **read** *swift for the open, brighteyed,*
3958.7	532.31	**for** *sticks, salmongaffs,* **read** *sticks, hayforks, salmongaffs,*
3968.5,10	533.9	**for** bar one. [...] bar one. **read** bar one! [...] bar one!
3980.8	533.21	**for** *nag. Cock* **read** *nag, Cock*
3986.1–2	533.28	**for** GANETT DEARY **read** GARRETT DEASY
3989.8	533.31–2	**run on** *Per vias rectas!* **following** *schooling gallop.)*
4002.5	534.10	**for** sort a **read** sort of a
4024.3	535.2	**for** *(Twirls around herself,* **read** *(Twirls round herself,*
4025.3–5	535.3	**for** dance? **read** dance? Clear the table.
4028.5	535.6	**for** *Zoe around the* **read** *Zoe round the*
4030.6	535.8	**for** *her around the* **read** *her round the*
4030.9–11	535.9	**transfer** *Bloom stands aside.* **to 535.8 following** *the room.*
4037.11– 4038.1	535.15	**for** *is a dahlia.* **read** *is an immense dahlia.*
4039.12	535.17	**for** *hand limply on* **read** *hand lightly on*
4044.4	535.22	**for** Lanner steps. So. **read** Lanner step. So.
4048.2	535.25–6	**for** *shrivels, shrinks, his* **read** *shrivels, sinks, his*
4049.3	535.27	**for** *time, pounds. Stephen* **read** *time, sounds. Stephen*

4050.3–5	535.28	**for** *fade, gold, rose, violet.*) **read** *fade, gold rosy violet.*)
4055.1	535.32	**for** *goldhaired, slim, in* **read** *goldhaired, slimsandalled, in*
4060.11	536.4	**for** evenly! *Balance!* **read** evenly! *Balancé!*
4081.4–7	536.25	**for** *hours steal* **read** *hours, one by one, steal*
4088.2	537.2	**for** (*Twisting, her* **read** (*Twirling, her*
4092.3	537.6	**for** *curtseying, twisting, simply* **read** *curtseying, twirling, simply*
4100.2	537.13–14	**for** *each with* **read** *each each with*
4100.10	537.14	**for** *movements, Stephen* **read** *movements. Stephen*
4117.1–5	538.2–3	**delete inset and run on** Come on all! **to follow** and through.
4133.1	538.18–19	**for** *they scotlootshoot lumbering* **read** *they scootlootshoot lumbering*
4141.1	538.26–7	**for** *piglings. Conmee* **read** *piglings, Conmee*
4144.3–4	538.29	**for** coffin. Steel **read** coffin steel
4148.8	539.2	**for** *last wiswitchback lumbering* **read** *last switchback lumbering*
4153.8	539.6	**for** *on wall. He* **read** *on walls. He*
4176.8	539.28	**for** you? What **read** you? No. What
4178.12,14	539.30–540.1	**for** Kinch killed her dosgbody bitchbody. She **read** Kinch dogsbody killed her bitchbody. She
4180.1–2	540.1	**for** *eyes into the* **read** *eyes on to the*
4186.10	540.8	**for** They said I **read** They say I

4214.4–6	541.6	**for** (*Panting.*) The **read** (*Panting.*) His noncorrosive sublimate! The
4219.4–6	541.10	**for** *outstretched fingers.*) Beware! God's **read** *outstretched finger.*) Beware God's
4220.1–2	541.10–11	**reposition** (*A green* [...] *Stephen's heart.*) **as a separate narrative direction**
4223.1–12	541.13	**in place of this line read** (*Strangled with rage, his features drawn grey and old.*) Shite!
4256.6	542.17	**for** *and flees from* **read** *and flies from*
4260.8	542.20	**for** *the halldoors. Lynch* **read** *the halldoor. Lynch*
4268.12–13	542.27	**for** *coattail.*) There. You **read** *coattail.*) Here, you
4279.5	543.10	**for** Didn't he ... ! **read** Didn't he ... ?
4284.3	543.15	**for** (*His hand under* **read** (*His head under*
4284.10	543.15	**for** *chain. Pulling, the* **read** *chain. Puling, the*
4290.16	543.21–2	**for** not a sixpenceworth **read** not sixpenceworth
4303.7–8	544.5	**for** here? Where **read** here or? Where
4306.12	544.8	**for** Oxford! (*Warningly.*) **read** Oxford? (*Warningly.*)
4308.6–7	544.10	**for** are you incog? **read** are. Incog!
4312.12	544.14	**for** *and shouts.*) That's **read** *and starts.*) That's
4322.4	544.23	**for** *a ghostly lewd* **read** *a ghastly lewd*
4330.7	544.31	**for** *trousers, follows from* **read** *trousers, follow from*

4336.6,8	545.4	**for** *leader: 65 C 66 C night* **read** *leader: 65 C, 66 C, night*
4340.1,3 4341.1	545.7–8	**for** *Garryowen, Whatdoyoucallhim, Strangeface, Fellowthatslike, Sawhimbefore, Chapwith, Chris* **read** *Garryowen, Whodoyoucallhim, Strangeface, Fellowthatsolike, Sawhimbefore, Chapwithawen, Chris*
4347.1–2	545.14–15	**for** *Holohan, man in the street, other man in the street, Footballboots,* **read** *Holohan, maninthestreet, othermaninthestreet, Footballboots,*
4354.1	545.21	**for** *Clonskea tram, the* **read** *Clonskeatram, the*
4356.8	545.23	**for** *Drimmie's, colonel* **read** *Drimmie's, Wetherup, colonel*
4364.4	545.30	**for** Hi! Stop him on **read** Hi! Stophim on
4366.9	545.32	**for** *noisy quarelling knot,* **read** *noisy quarrelling knot,*
4371.1	545.35–546.1	**for** guests. The uninvited. By **read** guests. Uninvited. By
4378.4–9	546.8	**for** didn't. The girls telling lies. He **read** didn't. I seen him. The girl there. He
4379.2,4	546.9	**for** up? Soldiers and civilians. **read** up? Soldier and civilian.
4381.15	546.11–12	**for** know and **read** know, and
4382.4	546.12	**for** man ran up **read** man run up
4387.5–7	546.15	**for** *of Kitty's and Lynch's heads.)* **read** *of Lynch's and Kitty's heads.)*
4388.7	546.16	**for** Poetic. Neopoetic. **read** Poetic. Uropoetic.

4384.1–4385.1	546.17–18	**transfer** VOICES Shesfaithfultheman. **(spelled thus in one word) to 546.13–14 following** shilling whore.
4396.2–4	546.26	**for** (*In* **read** (*Gentleman poet in*
4397.3	546.26	**for** *flowingbearded.*) Their's not **read** *flowingbearded.*) Theirs not
4405.11	547.6	**for** the private. **read** the privates.
4410.5	547.11	**for** *awry, advancing to* **read** *awry, advances to*
4413.4	547.14	**for** *up in the* **read** *up to the*
4429.2–3	547.30–31	**run on** (*He staggers a pace back.*) **as a speech direction following** perpendicular.
4435.3–4	548.6	**for** but modern philirenists, **read** but but human philirenists,
4439.14	548.10	**for** the college **read** the college.
4443.5	548.14	**for** with much marked **read** with such marked
4453.8	548.24	**for** *of Massachussets. He* **read** *of Massachusetts. He*
4462.7	549.2	**for** a back. **read** a bak.
4462.8–9, 4463.6–4464.2	549.2–5	**run on** (*He shakes* […] *and Lynch.*) **as a speech direction following** a back. **and position** (*General applause* […] *in acknowledgement.*) **as a separate narrative direction, inserting the two additonal parentheses**
4464.8	549.4	**for** *lifts the bucket* **read** *lifts his bucket*
4471.1	549.10–11	**for** patent medicine. A **read** patent medicines. A
4472.3–4	549.12	**for** country, suppose. (*He* **read** country. Suppose. (*He*

4474.7	549.14	**for** I don't want **read** I didn't want
4486.13	549.26	**for** saying. Taking a **read** saying. Taken a
4487.7–8	549.27	**for** absinthe, the greeneyed **read** absinthe. Greeneyed
4507.8	550.16	**for** *geese valant on* **read** *geese volant on*
4528.4	551.8	**for** the throat **read** the throats
4537.8	551.16	**for** *with a gladstone* **read** *with gladstone*
4541.10	551.20	**for** from the body **read** from body
4547.4–6	551.25	**for** hray ho rhother's hest **read** hray hor hother's hest.
4551.1	551.28–9	**for** *Mrs Mervy Talboys* **read** *Mrs Mervyn Talboys*
4555.5–6	552.1	**for** time as **read** time. As
4555.9	552.1	**for** to His Royal **read** to Her Royal
4586.3	552.30	**for** Strangers im my **read** Strangers in my
4597.13	553.11	**for** any bugger says **read** any fucker says
4620.1–4624.2	553.15–18	**transfer** THE CITIZEN *Erin go hragh!* (*Major Tweedy* […] *fierce hostility.*) **to 554.6–7 following** hashbaz. **and change** *hragh!* **in 553.16 to** *bragh!*
4613.8,4614.4	554.1–2	**for** *with epaulette, gilt chevrons and sabretache, his* **read** *with epaulettes, gilt chevrons and sabretaches, his*
4618.12	554.5	**for** them! Mahal shalal **read** them! Mahar shalal

63

4628.2	554.10	**for** (*Waves the* **read** (*Moves the*
4664.1	555.16–17	**for** *bawl Whores* **read** *bawl. Whores*
4672.10	555.25	**for** *a noisless yawn.* **read** *a noiseless yawn.*
4680.6	555.32	**for** *rains dragon's teeth.* **read** *rains dragons' teeth.*
4682.12	556.2	**for** *Wolfe Tome against* **read** *Wolfe Tone against*
4688.2	556.7	**for** *The Donoghue. On* **read** *The O'Donoghue. On*
4693.10	556.12	**for** *a long petticoat* **read** *a lace petticoat*
4705.7	556.24	**for** *celebrant's petticoats, revealing* **read** *celebrant's petticoat, revealing*
4708.2	556.27	**for** Htengier Lnetopinmo Dog **read** Htengier Tnetopinmo Dog
4722.1–13	557.10–11	**transfer** (*The retriever* […] *barks noisily.*) **from 558.15 to follow** fucking windpipe!
4736.1–4739.4	557.11–14	**transfer** OLD GUMMY […] take him! **to 557.27–8 following** pure reason.
4747.6	558.5	**for** *Stephen, fists outstretched,* **read** *Stephen, fist outstretched,*
4757.11	558.14	**for** him! he's fainted! **read** him! He's fainted!
4770.6–7	559.2	**for** Here bugger off, Harry. There's the **read** Here. Bugger off, Harry. Here's the
4771.1–2	559.2–3	**reposition** (*Two raincaped* […] *the group.*) **as a separate narrative direction following** the cops.
4775.5–6,9–10	559.7	**for** lady and he insulted us and assaulted **read** lady. And he insulted us. And assaulted

4793.12	559.25	**for** Bennett'll have you **read** Bennett'll shove you
4799.2	560.5	**for** (*Taking out* **read** (*Takes out*
4814.6	560.20	**for** cup. Throwaway. (*He* **read** cup. *Throwaway.* (*He*
4856.1–2	562.2	**reposition** (*They move* [...] *heavy tread.*) **as a separate narrative direction following** gentlemen.
4863.3–4	562.8–9	**for** grief and **read** grief. And
4883.8	562.29	**for** a specialty. Will **read** a speciality. Will
4888.5	563.4	**for** *Bloom in* **read** *Bloom, in*
4930.2,6–7	564.16	**for** (*Groans.*) Who? Black panther vampire. **read** (*Frowns.*) Who? Black panther. Vampire.
4938.5	564.23	**for** *light hands and* **read** *light hand and*
4943.4–5	564.28	**for** dim ... **read** dim sea.
4945.2	564.29–30	**for** *holding his hat* **read** *holding the hat*
4951.7	565.4	**for** him ... (*He* **read** him. (*He*
4967.4	565.20	**for** *white lambskin peeps* **read** *white lambkin peeps*

16: Eumaeus

6.13	569.6	**for** no pumps of **read** no pump of
19.1, 20.11	569.17–19	**transfer** brushing **from 569.19 to 569.17 and read** preliminaries as brushing, in spite [...] shaving line, they both
33.10	570.3	**for** by Mullet's and **read** by Mullett's and

59.3–4	570.27	**for** bread? At **read** bread at
67.10	570.35	**for** little juijitsu for **read** little jiujitsu for
70.7	571.1	**for** unconscious that, but **read** unconscious but
74.12	571.5	**for** or Malony which **read** or Mahony which
95.1	571.24	**for** others pratically. Most **read** others practically. Most
98.6–7	571.28	**for** Judas, said Stephen, who **read** Judas, Stephen said, who
101.12	571.31	**for** bridge when a **read** bridge where a
109.7	572.1–2	**for** a quondam friend **read** a *quondam* friend
114.1, 115.1	572.6	**transfer** *Night!* **to a separate line with a dialogue dash and in roman not italic, and begin a new paragraph with** Stephen, of
116.10	572.7–8	**for** delicacy, inamsuch as **read** delicacy, inasmuch as
119.6	572.10	**for** least. Although unusual **read** least. Though unusual
121.6	572.12	**for** be about waylaying **read** be abroad waylaying
129.6	572.19	**for** in any over **read** in an over
136.1,3	572.25	**enclose** though not proved **in parentheses, not commas**
138.13–139.8	572.28	**for** relative had **read** relative, a woman, as the tale went, of extreme beauty, had
146.10	572.34	**for** with Leneban and **read** with Lenehan and
147.9–11	572.35	**for** sprinkling of **read** sprinkling of a number of

157.5,6	573.7	**for** job to morrow or the next **read** job tomorrow or next
161.12–14	573.11	**for** laugh, Got **read** laugh. I got
176.1	573.24–5	**for** *disco,* etcetera, as **read** *disco, etcetera,* as
181.7–8	573.29–30	**for** needful – whereas. He **read** needful. Whereas. He
186.3	573.34	**for** his invetiongstia. He **read** his investigation. He
190.2–3	574.1	**for** recollect about **read** recollect. About
191.1–3	574.2	**for** them, or **read** them he wondered, or
195.13	574.6	**for** Stephen lent **read** Stephen anyhow lent
197.11	574.8–9	**for** back some time. **read** back one time.
221.9	574.32	**for** impecuniosity. Probably he **read** impecuniosity. Palbably he
233.1–2	575.7	**for** – He's down **read** – He is down
245.1	575.19	**for** – Needs, Mr **read** – Needs! Mr
247.7	575.21	**for** needs and everyone **read** needs or everyone
262.1	575.36	**for** quite legitimately, out **read** quite legitimate, out
267.6–9	576.4	**for** confusion. **read** confusion, which they did.
282.9	576.19	**for** on through in **read** on though in
309.7	577.8	**for** urinal he perceived **read** urinal they perceived
314.1	577.12	**for** – *Putanna madonna,* **read** – *Puttana madonna,*

317.1	577.14–15	**insert speech** – *Mezzo.*
319.1–6	577.15–16	**insert speech** – *Ma ascolta! Cinque la testa più* ...
324.6–7	577.20	**for** he wouldn't vouch **read** he could not vouch
336.7	577.31	**for** cursory examinatiou, turned **read** cursory examination, turned
339.11	577.35	**no new paragraph at** Mr Bloom,
342.14–343.1	577.37–578.1	**for** voice, *apropos* of **read** voice, *à propos* of
347.1–2	578.5	**for** *Belladonna voglio.* **read** *Belladonna. Voglio.*
349.1	578.6–7	**for** from dead lassitude **read** from lassitude
362.4–5	578.20	**for** impostures, Stephens aid after **read** impostures, Stephen said after
363.3,6,9	578.21	**full stops, not commas, after** Podmore [...] Goodbody [...] Doyle
393.1	579.13	**for** – Bottle out **read** – Bottles out
398.1, 401.1	579.18,21	**for** – Pom, he **read** – Pom! he **(twice)**
402.1	579.22	**delete dialogue dash**
415.7–8	579.36	**for** continued, W.B. **read** continued, D.B.
419.4–11	580.3	**for** from. My **read** from. I belongs there. That's where I hails from. My
430.11	580.14	**for** he finelly did **read** he finally did
437.1	580.20	**for** father. Boo! The **read** father. Broo! The
440.3	580.23	**for** husband, W.B. **read** husband, D.B.
443.13	580.26	**for** about you, do you? **read** about you?

452.5–6	580.35	**for** See? W.B. **read** See? D.B.
454.6	580.37	**for** his neighbours a **read** his neighbour a
460.5–11	581.5	**for** America. I **read** America. We was chased by pirates one voyage. I
463.6	581.7	**for** *Gospodi pomilooy.* That's **read** *Gospodi pomilyou.* That's
475.5,8	581.20	**for** attention on the scene exhibited, at a **read** attention at the scene exhibited, a
479.4	581.24	**for** day long, the **read** day, the
481.3	581.26	**for** them there **read** them sitting there
484.9	581.29	**for** inquired genially. **read** inquired generally.
491.1	581.35	**new paragraph at** Though not
508.9	582.15	**for** the ouside, considering **read** the outside, considering
515.6	582.22	**for** improvement tower **read** improvement, tower
541.7	583.11	**for** for a matter **read** for the matter
543.2–3	583.13	**for** always cooped **read** always and ever cooped
568.11–12	583.37	**for** card picture and **read** card, picture, and
573.12	584.4	**for** the Chinese does. **read** the Chinks does.
585.1	584.15	**new paragraph, with dialogue dash, at** That's a
594.3	584.25	**for** Mr Bloom and **read** Mr B. and
600.9	584.31	**for** very. **read** very!
601.11	584.32	**for** reading by fits **read** reading in fits

606.1	584.36	**for** yesterday, some **read** yesterday, roughly some
618.8–9	585.11	**for** Mr Bloom interpolated. Can **read** Mr B. interrogated. Can
632.3	585.23–4	**for** quite obviously at **read** quite obliviously at
641.6–7	585.32–3	**for** that sortof onus **read** that sort of onus
643.15	585.35	**for** a very laudable **read** a highly laudable
662.15	586.15–16	**for** a a strong **read** a strong
672.4	586.24	**for** buggers. Sucks your **read** buggers. Suck your
673.10	586.25	**for** he accomodatingly dragged **read** he accommodatingly dragged
681.10–682.1	586.33–4	**for** the someway **read** the. Someway
694.5–6	587.8	**for** work, longshoreman one said. **read** work, one longshoreman said.
699.5	587.13	**for** number. A **read** number. Ate. A
716.7	587.30	**for** admit that he **read** admit he
740.2	588.17	**for** said that it **read** said it
768.7–11	589.8	**for** man I mean. The **read** man, I mean, the
785.11–12	589.25	**for** it and **read** it. And
788.8	589.27	**for** his mentlal organs **read** his mental organs
809.4–11	590.11	**for** puddle – it clopped out of it when taken up – by **read** puddle it clopped out of when taken up by
815.8	590.17	**for** But oblige **read** But O, oblige
854.4–5	591.19	**for** outline, the **read** outline of the

871.11	591.35	**for** succulent tuckink with **read** succulent tuckin with
906.11	592.33	**for** wreck of Daunt's **read** wreck off Daunt's
911.8–9	593.1	**for** the Irish *Times*) **read** the *Irish Times*)
933.4	593.23	**for** exploit, gazing up **read** exploit, gaping up
938.12	593.28	**for** himself close at **read** himself closer at
940.6	593.30	**for** apparently woke a **read** apparently awoke a
940.12	593.30–31	**no new paragraph at** A hoof
943.1–2	593.33	**for** corporation, who, **read** corporation stones, who,
948.8	594.1	**for** hard times in **read** hard lines in
966.11–12	594.18	**for** Ask her captain, **read** Ask the then captain,
983.5	594.35	**for** the redoutable specimen **read** the redoubtable specimen
985.2	595.2–3	**no new paragraph at** Skin-the-Goat,
990.2	595.7	**for** million pounds' worth **read** million pounds worth
996.7	595.13–14	**for** in Cavan growing **read** in Navan growing
1049.2	596.28–9	**for** he (Bloom) couldn't **read** he (B.) couldn't
1052.10	596.32	**for** Dannyman coning forward **read** Dannyman coming forward
1060.1,12	597.2–3	**enclose** though, personally […] such thing **in parentheses**
1063.9	597.6	**for** (he man having **read** (he having
1066.6	597.8–9	**for** nicknamed Skin-the-Goat, merely **read** nicknamed Skin-the, merely

1082.2	597.24	**for** whole eventempored person **read** whole eventempered person
1091.7	597.33	**for** a noncommital accent, **read** a noncommittal accent,
1094.4	597.36	**for** Mr Bloom proceeded **read** Mr B. proceeded
1099.11	598.4	**for** violence or intolerance **read** violence and intolerance
1106.1	598.11	**delete dialogue dash**
1107.8	598.12	**for** was overwhelmingly full **read** was full
1116.2	598.21	**for** accuse – remarked **read** accuse, remarked
1117.1	598.21	**new paragraph at** He turned
1124.7–1125.1	598.29	**for** are practical **read** are imbued with the proper spirit. They are practical
1138.11	599.5–6	**for** a small smattering **read** a smattering
1139.3	599.6	**for** classical day in **read** classical days in
1139.8	599.6	**for** *vita beni.* Where **read** *vita bene.* Where
1148.8	599.15	**for** meaning to work. **read** meaning work.
1176.3	600.5	**for** then which some **read** then with some
1177.8	600.6	**for** Mr Bloom attached **read** Mr B attached
1178.14	600.7–8	**for** the the right **read** the right
1197.7–8	600.26	**for** and esthetesand the **read** and esthetes and the
1216.10	601.9	**for** was interest **read** was his interest
1235.10	601.28	**for** addressed to A. **read** addressed A.

1242.4–10	601.35	**for** Ascot *Throwaway* **read** Ascot meeting, the Gold Cup. Victory of outsider *Throwaway*
1243.6	601.35	**for** when Captain Marshall's **read** when Capt. Marshall's
1248.5	602.3	**for** put in, **read** put it in,
1252.4	602.6	**for** *as great* **read** *as a great*
1254.4,13	602.8–9	**transfer** *by* **to precede the parenthesis, and read** *out by* (certainly [...] Corny) *Messrs.*
1256.8	602.11	**for** *law), John Henry* **read** *law), Jno. Henry*
1257.8	602.11	**for** *Power eatondph 1/8* **read** *Power, .)eatondph 1/8*
1259.7–8	602.13	**for** *Dedalus, B.A.,* **read** *Dedalus, Stephen Dedalus, B.A.,*
1259.11	602.13	**for** *A., Edward J.* **read** *A., Edw. J.*
1260.4	602.14	**for** *Cornelius Kelleher,* **read** *Cornelius T. Kelleher,*
1260.10	602.14	**for** *L. Bloom, C.P.* **read** *L. Boom, C.P.*
1262.6–7	602.16	**for** by *L. Boom* (as **read** by L. Boom (as
1273.8–9	602.27	**for** managing the thing, there. **read** managing to. There.
1277.1–2	602.30–31	**for** his side-value 1,000 **read** his side. Value 1,000
1277.10–11	602.31	**for** added for **read** added. For
1278.9, 1279.4	602.32–3	**for** by *Rightaway,* 5 yrs, 9st 4lbs, Thrale (W. **read** by *Rightaway– Thrale,* 5 yrs, 9st 4lbs, (W.

1280.7	602.34	**for** 3. Bettings 5 **read** 3. Betting 5
1284.11	602.37	**for** filly Sceptre on **read** filly *Sceptre* on
1285.5	603.1	**for** by Braine so **read** by Braime so
1287.2	603.2	**for** with 300 in **read** with 3,000 in
1295.10–11	603.10	**for** that, Mr Bloom said. **read** that, he, Bloom, said.
1297.1	603.12	**delete dialogue dash**
1302.3	603.16–17	**for** a fiinger at **read** a finger at
1318.6	603.33	**for** a fortinght was **read** a fortnight was
1333.5	604.10	**for** title *rôle* how **read** title role how
1337.6	604.14	**for** frigid expression notwithstanding **read** frigid exterior notwithstanding
1349.8	604.26	**for** course, Mr Bloom **read** course, as Bloom
1355.7–12	604.32	**for** her. I **read** her. She loosened many a man's thighs. I
1356.7	604.32–3	**for** barber's. Her husband **read** barber's. The husband
1365.6	605.4–5	**for** till it bit **read** till bit
1368.3,5	605.7	**for** upon encouraging his downfal though **read** upon encompassing his downfall though
1371.5	605.10	**for** declared favorite, where **read** declared favourite, where
1378.4	605.17	**for** fact that the **read** fact the
1386.5	605.25	**for** folk? Though **read** folk? Poser. Though
1400.2	606.1	**for** his head-much in **read** his head much in
1402.1	606.3	**for** And the coming **read** And then coming

74

1411.14– 1412.5	606.13	**for** Stephen. And, **read** Stephen, about blood and the sun. And,
1423.8–10	606.23	**for** contents rapidly, **read** contents it contained rapidly,
1438.10–11	606.37	**for** about '96. Very **read** about ninety six. Very
1452.11– 1454.5	607.13–14	**for** rest, yes, Puritanism. It does though, St Joseph's sovereign … whereas no **read** rest. Yes, puritanisme, it does though Saint Joseph's sovereign thievery alors (Bandez!) Figne toi trop. Whereas no
1467.5	607.26	**for** possible embarrassement while **read** possible embarrassment while
1491.2	608.12	**for** Proctor to **read** Proctor tries to
1495.7	608.16	**for** He, Bloom, enjoyed **read** He B, enjoyed
1497.2	608.18	**for** historic *fracas* when **read** historic fracas when
1500.4–5	608.21	**for** the prinitng worsk of **read** the printing works of
1504.3	608.25–6	**for** mudslinging occuaption, reflecting **read** mudslinging occupation, reflecting
1517.14– 1518.2	609.2	**for** time, being **read** time all the same being
1530.4	609.13	**for** the cabmen and **read** the cabman and
1557.4	610.1–2	**for** when when Miss **read** when Miss
1569.9–10	610.14	**for** eat, were **read** eat, even were
1575.1	610.19	**for** – Yesterday, exclaimed **read** – Yesterday! exclaimed
1578.8	610.22	**for** Bloom, reflected. **read** Bloom reflected.
1592.5	610.35	**for** step further than **read** step farther than

1594.12–14	610.37–611.1	**for** fashion at **read** fashion by our friend at
1603.4	611.8	**for** weighing the **read** weighing up the
1619.8	611.23	**for** to pu coin **read** to put coin
1624.1–2	611.28	**for** failed top erceive any **read** failed to perceive any
1635.3	612.1	**for** of pottheen and **read** of potheen and
1636.5	612.2	**for** let XX equal **read** let X equal
1648.11	612.14	**for** keeper, of **read** keeper of
1652.10	612.18	**for** his (Bloom's) busy **read** his (B's) busy
1680.1	613.8–9	**for** speaking, *The* **read** speaking. *The*
1682.1	613.11	**for** Thereupon he **read** Hereupon he
1692.5	613.20	**for** his feet so **read** his seat so
1699.8	613.26–7	**for** opposite to him **read** opposite him
1710.1	613.37	**for** down on **read** down, on
1714.5–8	614.4	**for** around nimbly, considering frankly, at **read** around, nimbly considering, frankly at
1715.15, 1716.1	614.5–6	**for** bye the right **read** bye, his right
1733.3	614.24	**for** they passed on **read** they turned on
1765.6	615.18	**for** whom Bloom did **read** whom B. did
1771.3	615.24	**for** the swing chain, a **read** the swingchains, a
1778.9	615.30	**for** usual plucked **read** usual, plucked
1780.6	615.32	**for** peril to night. Beware **read** peril tonight. Beware
1789.8–9	616.4	**for** big foolish nervous noodly **read** big nervous foolish noodly

1810.8	616.25	**for** on a air **read** on an air
1812.12–13	616.27	**for** of *Johannes Jeep* about **read** of Johannes Jeep about
1840.8	617.18–19	**for** the pecuniar y emolument **read** the pecuniary emolument
1843.12–13	617.22	**for** time but **read** time. But
1859.9–10	617.37	**for** fellows and **read** fellows. And
1863.1	618.3–4	**for** derogatory what soever as **read** derogatory whatsoever as
1885.10–11	618.26	**for** indifferent. He merely **read** indifferent, but merely
1886.5–11	618.27	as he sat on his lowbacked car, **in italic, not roman**
1893.12	618.34	**for** his sest near **read** his seat near

17: Ithaca

24.7	619.23	**for** orthodox religions, national, **read** orthodox religious, national,
30.11	620.4–5	**for** Bloom assently covertly **read** Bloom assented covertly
53.4	620.26–7	**for** 1886 occusionally with **read** 1886 occasionally with
58.6	620.31	**for** Julius Mastiansky, **read** Julius (Juda) Mastiansky,
93.6	621.31	**for** Francis Frœdman, pharmaceutical **read** Francis Froedman, pharmaceutical
111.1–5	622.15–16	**for** candle, a **read** candle of 1 CP, a

112.6	622.17	**for** candle of 1 CP. **read** candle.
141.3–148.2	623.11	**for** Island: of **read** Island: of his aunt Sara, wife of Richie (Richard) Goulding, in the kitchen of their lodgings at 62 Clanbrassil street: of
165.1	623.33	**for** of 2.400 million **read** of 2,400 million
177.7	624.12	**for** 1893) particulary as **read** 1893) particularly as
179.13	624.14	**for** of 20.000 gallons **read** of 20,000 gallons
187.1	624.21–2	**for** its umplumbed profundity **read** its unplumbed profundity
187.11	624.22–3	**for** exceeding 8.000 fathoms: **read** exceeding 8,000 fathoms:
196.4	624.31	**for** its luteosfulvous bed: **read** its luteofulvous bed:
198.8–199.5	624.33	**for** peninsulas and **read** peninsulas and islands, its persistent formation of homothetic islands, peninsulas and
210.5–7	625.7	**for** by the **read** by the well by the
216.2	625.13	**for** its infaillibity as **read** its infallibility as
222.10–223.1	625.20	**for** rivers, ifnavigable, floating **read** rivers, if navigable, floating
265.7	626.27	**for** the course of **read** the source of
301.5	627.30	**for** purse dispaying coins, **read** purse displaying coins,
302.2	627.30	**for** aromatic violet comfits. **read** aromatic (violet) comfits.
303.10–11	627.32	**for** black olivesin oleaginous **read** blakc olives in oleaginous

310.1	628.6	**for** one the **read** one, the
318.1	628.13	**for** jamjars of **read** jamjars (empty) of
321.3–4	628.17	**for** 8 87, 8 86. **read** 8 87, 88 6.
333.11–12	628.29	**for** W Sweny **read** W.Sweny
394.9–10	630.24	**for** respectively by **read** respectively for competition by
411.5	631.8	**for** Marion Tweedy **read** Marion (Molly) Tweedy
423.5–11	631.21–2	**transfer** produced by R.Shelton 26 December 1892 **to 631.20 and read** *Sailor* (produced [...] 1892, written [...] Miss Whelan under the
429.1	631.25–6	**for** the anticipatep diamond **read** the anticipated diamond
443.3	632.5	**for** rhymes homophonous **read** rhymes, homophonous
445.5	632.6–7	**for** new sollicitorgeneral, Dunbar **read** new solicitorgeneral, Dunbar
451.7–8	632.13	**for** according arbitrary as future **read** according as arbitrary future
467.10	632.29	**for** house. Medina **read** house, Medina
470.6	632.32	**for** the cofferoom of **read** the coffeeroom of
479.2–3	633.7	**for** Riordan, a **read** Riordan (Dante), a
502.5–6	633.28–9	**for** round precipitous **read** round and round precipitous
512.3	634.6	**for** indoor exercices, formerly **read** indoor exercises, formerly
517.5–8	634.11	**for** pleasant relaxation **read** pleasant rigidity, a more pleasant relaxation

528.6–7	634.20	**for** Bloom about **read** Bloom and Bloom's thoughts about
535.1	634.27–8	**for** (subsequently Rudolf Bloom) **read** (subsequently Rudolph Bloom)
535.4	634.28	**for** of Szombathely, Vienna, **read** of Szombathély, Vienna,
543.6	635.4	**for** Saint Nicolas Without, **read** Saint Nicholas Without,
553.3	635.14	**for** arts second **read** arts, second
579.9	636.7	**for** waxwork exhihition at **read** waxwork exhibition at
601.2	636.29	**for** 4 oz., pots, **read** 4 oz. pots,
604.9	636.32–3	**for** Trumplee. Montpat. Plamtroo. **read** Trumplee. Moutpat. Plamtroo.
619.7–620.2	637.15–16	**for** Queen's hotel, Queen's hotel Queen's Ho ... **read** Queen's Hotel, Queen's Hotel, Queen's Hotel. Queen's Ho ...
631.3,6	637.27	**for** aforesaid), the toxin aforesaid, at **read** aforesaid, the toxin aforesaid), at
648.1	638.9	**for** model pedagogie themes **read** model pedagogic themes
656.3	638.17	**for** sunrise, 3.33 **read** sunrise 3.33
724.2	640.16	**for** What fragment of **read** What fragments of
733.1–2	640.25	**insert, and begin the paragraph with,** By juxtaposition.
734.3	640.25	**transfer** entitled **to 640.26 to follow** style,
739.4	640.30	**for** substituted goph, explaining **read** substituted qoph, explaining
748.9	641.8	**for** having taught **read** having been taught

759.7	641.19	**for** in Chanan David **read** in Chanah David
786.4,6	642.14	**for** The Traditionnal accent af the **read** The traditional accent of the
793.4	642.21	**for** exemplars Charles **read** exemplars, Charles
799.3	642.27	**for** a mechianacal mixture, **read** a mechanical mixture,
805.4–6	643.5	**for** *it ow'er the je's garden* **read** *it o'er the jew's garden*
813.3	644.2	**for** *out came* **read** *out there came*
845.1	645.13–14	**for** the incitation of **read** the incitations of
870.2–3	646.6–7	**for** proximate, ahallucination, lieutenant **read** proximate, a hallucination, lieutenant
873.10–874.3	646.10	**for** intervals to **read** intervals to more distant intervals to
907.11	647.13	**for** unexpectedness, were differences **read** unexpectedness, their differences
909.8	647.14	**for** gifts 1) an **read** gifts (1) an
915.6–7	647.20	**for** positions clockwise of moveable **read** positions of clockwise moveable
926.4	647.30–31	**for** him not for her **read** him to her
933.5	648.5	**for** and immediateiy adjacent **read** and immediately adjacent
936.1,4	648.7–8	**for** a prolungation of such extemporisation? **read** a prolongation of such an extemporisation?
952.3–5	648.24	**for** Mary Goulding, 26 **read** Mary Dedalus (born Goulding), 26

958.5–6	648.30	**for** seven shilling, advanced **read** seven shillings sterling, advanced
976.8–9	649.16	**for** Dublin, anintuitive parti coloured clown **read** Dublin, an intuitive particoloured clown
999.2	650.7	**for** menstruation, of **read** menstruation of
1003.3	650.10–11	**for** catastrophic cataclyms which **read** catastrophic cataclysms which
1009.4	650.17	**for** in place **read** in the place
1024.1, 1027.1	650.31,33	**position** borne by [...] borne by **as separate lines, centred**
1030.7	651.2	**for** *exitu Israël de* **read** *exitu Israel de*
1032.4	651.4	**for** each so at **read** each do at
1041.4	651.13	**for** various constellation? **read** various constellations?
1047.4	651.19	**for** 000, miles) **read** 000 miles)
1053.6	651.24	**for** evermoving from **read** evermoving wanderers from
1055.1	651.26	**for** years, threscore and **read** years, threescore and
1083.5	652.19	**for** the problem of **read** the problems of
1090.5	652.26	**for** and statosphere was **read** and stratosphere was
1097.5,7	652.32–3	**for** forms wiih finite différences resulting **read** forms with finite differences resulting
1108.9	653.8	**for** the interdependant gyrations **read** the interdependent gyrations
1115.8	653.14–15	**for** younger satroscopist: the **read** younger astroscopist: the

1124.4	653.23	**for** but lesser **read** but of lesser
1125.1	653.23	**for** and dissapeared from **read** and disappeared from
1132.1	653.30	**for** persons, the **read** persons: the
1135.1	653.33	**for** animals, persistance of **read** animals, persistence of
1145.3	654.6	**transfer** probable **to 654.9 following** its
1161.8	654.24	**for** rising, and **read** rising and
1171.9	655.1–2	**for** Stephen's gaze? **read** Stephen's, gaze?
1177.10	655.7	**for** invisible person, **read** invisible attractive person,
1194.4	655.23	**for** letter who **read** letter, who
1198.9	655.27	**for** insistent vescical pressure. **read** insistent vesical pressure.
1203.12	655.32	**for** circumcised (1st January, **read** circumcised (1 January,
1239.2–5	657.5	**transfer** Ned Lambert (in bed), **to precede** Tom Kernan (in bed),
1278.1	658.11–12	**for** of anetcedent sensations **read** of antecedent sensations
1280.1	658.13	**for** furniture? **read** furniture.
1310.3	659.8	**for** sustained, pedal, **read** sustained pedal,
1314.3	659.13	**for** and slender **read** and a slender
1321.6	659.20	**for** on tbe majolicatopped **read** on the majolicatopped
1331.1	659.30	**for** That truncated **read** The truncated

1337.7–8	660.3	**for** under a ransparent bellshade, **read** under a transparent bellshade,
1369.1–5	661.6–7	**insert additional entry** *The Beauties of Killarney* (wrappers).
1381.1	661.19	**for** Lockart's *Life* **read** Lockhart's *Life*
1385.7	661.23	**for** *War* (bronw cloth, **read** *War* (brown cloth,
1386.4	661.24	**for** Library Governor's **read** Library, Governor's
1395.10	662.1	**for** missing recurrent **read** missing, recurrent
1399.5	662.5	**for** into Engflih by **read** into Englifh by
1454.1	663.29	**for** occasion (10 October **read** occasion (17 October
1476.2	664.24	**for** BALANCE .... 0.16.6 **read** BALANCE 0.17.5
1480.5	664.28	**for** benignant persistant ache **read** benignant persistent ache
1486.13	664.34	**for** right and, **read** right foot and,
1491.6	664.38	**for** lacerated unguial fragment. **read** lacerated unguical fragment.
1494.1	665.2–3	**for** other unguial fragments, **read** other unguical fragments,
1516.3	665.24	**for** than 5 minutes **read** than 15 minutes
1517.10	665.25	**for** to ressemble the **read** to resemble the
1523.7	665.30–31	**for** Encyclopaedia Brittanica and **read** Encyclopaedia Britannica and
1534.7	666.5	**for** with a fingertame **read** with fingertame
1541.10	666.12	**for** tierod brace, **read** tierod and brace,

1546.12	666.17	**for** service, pantry, **read** service), pantry,
1556.1	666.24–5	**for** tulips blue **read** tulips, blue
1557.3,4,10	666.25–6	**for** valley, [bulbs obtainable, from [...] Limited)] wholesale **read** valley (bulbs obtainable from [...] Limited) wholesale
1558.6,8,9	666.27	**for** bulb merchant and nurseryman, agent for **read** bulb merchants and nurserymen, agents for
1567.5	667.1	**for** be subsquently introduced? **read** be subsequently introduced?
1599.6	667.32	**for** Indoor discussion **read** Indoor: discussion
1611.5	668.12	**for** classical moto (*Semper* **read** classical motto (*Semper*
1613.1–2	668.13–14	**for** L.L.D. *honoris causa*, Bloomville, **read** L.L.D. (*honoris causa*), Bloomville,
1634.10	669.1	**for** youth? **read** youth.
1654.2	669.20	**for** (2 Febuary 1888) **read** (2 February 1888)
1655.2	669.21	**for** of 20.000 torchbearers, **read** of 20,000 torchbearers,
1655.10	669.22	**for** bearing 2.000 torches **read** bearing 2,000 torches
1656.10	669.22–3	**for** and John **read** and (honest) John
1660.2	669.27	**for** £60 par annum, **read** £60 per annum,
1661.10	669.28	**for** of £1.200 (estimate **read** of £1,200 (estimate
1662.5	669.29	**for** 20 years purchase) **read** 20 years' purchase)

1680.4–8	670.10–11	**for** or unpressed posrage stamps (7 shilling, mauve, **read** or impressed postage stamps (7 schilling, mauve,
1683.2	670.13	**for** 1878, antique **read** 1878), antique
1687.3	670.17	**for** a commestible fowl). **read** a comestible fowl).
1690.1	670.20	**for** of £5.000.000 stg **read** of £5,000,000 stg
1692.9–10	670.23	**for** delivery at **read** delivery per delivery at
1697.3	670.27	**for** premium £1.000.000 sterling. **read** premium £1,000,000 sterling.
1707.6	671.2	**for** by 4.386.035 the **read** by 4,386,035 the
1708.2	671.2	**for** according the census **read** according to census
1714.9	671.9	**for** of 500.00 W.H.P. **read** of 500,000 W.H.P.
1723.9, 1724.6	671.18	**enclose** 10/– per [...] (trilingual) included **in parentheses, not square brackets**
1733.4	671.26–7	**for** Lancashire Yorkshire **read** Lancashire and Yorkshire
1752.2	672.9	**for** What eventually would **read** What eventuality would
1757.10	672.14	**for** night allievated fatigue **read** night alleviated fatigue
1766.2	672.23	**for** The commital of **read** The committal of
1770.13	672.27–8	**for** in wonders a **read** in wonder, a
1795.9–1796.8	673.21	**for** deceased: 3 **read** deceased: a cameo scarfpin, property of Rudolph Bloom (born Virag), deceased: 3
1814.11–13	674.1	**for** boots: a1d. ad hesive stamp, **read** boots: a 1d. adhesive stamp,

1815.11	674.2	**for** of measurements **read** of the measurements
1816.3	674.2–3	**for** compiled, before, **read** compiled before,
1816.9	674.3	**for** 2 months of **read** 2 months' of
1821.9	674.8	**for** addressed to **read** addressed (erroneously) to
1822.9	674.8–9	**for** commencing: Dear **read** commencing (erroneously): Dear
1827.7–8	674.13	**for** way insuring, instant **read** way, insuring instant
1850.11	675.2–3	**for** the most immediate **read** the not immediate
1856.8	675.8	**for** Scottish Widow's Assurance **read** Scottish Widows' Assurance
1857.2	675.8–9	**for** intestated Millcent (Milly) **read** intestated Millicent (Milly)
1875.3	675.27	**for** indistinct daguerrotype of **read** indistinct daguerreotype of
1878.1	675.29–30	**for** ancient hagadah book **read** ancient haggadah book
1882.10	676.1	**for** those four whole **read** those five whole
1884.1	676.3–4	**for** be … wlth your **read** be … with your
1889.3–6	676.9	**for** man widower, unkempt hair, **read** man, widower, unkempt of hair,
1892.1	676.12	**for** septuagenarian suicide **read** septuagenarian, suicide
1901.1	676.20–21	**for** the tetragrammation: the **read** the tetragrammaton: the
1924.8	677.11	**for** of grooseberry fool **read** of gooseberry fool

1965.5,9	678.20	**for** reunite, for increase and multiplication which **read** reunite for increase and multiplication, which
1976.6	678.29	**for** of Tiperrary, the **read** of Tipperary, the
1982.4	679.4	**for** Jerusalem, tbe holy **read** Jerusalem, the holy
1984.8–9	679.6	**for** statues, nude **read** statues of nude
1993.12	679.15	**for** Ursa Major produced **read** Ursa Maior produced
1996.4	679.17–18	**for** Ursa Major. On **read** Ursa Maior. On
1996.11	679.18	**for** moon, reveated in **read** moon, revealed in
2002.9	679.23	**for** Bloom Leopold **read** Bloom, Leopold
2017.1,3	680.5	**for** imperceptibly hea would her and **read** imperceptibly he would hear and
2030.3	680.17	**for** invisible the **read** invisible: the
2031:1	680.17–18	**for** perilous the **read** perilous: the
2049.2	681.2–3	**for** row, Merchants Arch, **read** row, Merchants' Arch,
2064.2	681.17	**for** multiform mutitudinous garments, **read** multiform, multitudinous garments,
2071.10–2078.2	681.23	**for** walking, silently, **read** walking, charged with collected articles of recently disvested male wearing apparel, silently,
2078.5	681.29	**for** divinities, to **read** divinities: to
2088.9–10	682.8	**for** Great Nothern Railway Amiens **read** Great Northern Railway, Amiens
2096.6	682.16	**for** border, a accordion **read** border, an accordion

2130.1	683.16	**for** whereas, he **read** whereas he
2151.1	684.4–5	**for** transmitted first **read** transmitted, first
2164.8, 2165.1	684.18–19	**for** between agents and reagents at **read** between agent(s) and reagent(s) at
2178.2	684.32	**for** As natural **read** As as natural
2190.11	685.11	**for** other altered processes **read** other parallel processes
2205.5–2206.1	685.25	**for** impossibly. If **read** impossibly. Hushmoney by moral influence, possibly. If
2209.7	685.28–9	**for** protecting separator **read** protecting the separator
2212.6	685.32	**for** hymen, the **read** hymen: the
2216.4	686.1–2	**for** female, the **read** female: the
2227.10	686.12–13	**for** reflections reduced **read** reflections, reduced
2232.4–5	686.17	**for** adipose posterior **read** adipose anterior and posterior
2239.2	686.23	**for** revelation; a **read** revelation: a
2260.4,7	687.10–11	**for** anonymous, author a gentlemen of **read** anonymous author a gentleman of
2275.2–4	687.25	**for** celebrated 2 calendar months after **read** celebrated 1 calendar month after
2281.12	687.31	**for** January 1895, aged **read** January 1894, aged
2289.9	688.4–5	**for** which in **read** which, in
2303.1,6	688.18	**for** Listener: S. [...] Narrator N. **read** Listener, S. [...] Narrator, N.
2316.12	688.31	**for** depicted on a **read** depicted in a

| 2329.1–2 | 689.10–11 | **for** auk's eggin the **read** auk's egg in the |

18: Penelope

4.4	690.4	**for** interesting to that **read** interesting for that
10.11	690.10	**for** wear I **read** wear them I
40.9	691.12	**for** Pooles Myriorana and **read** Pooles Myriorama and
47.12	691.19	**for** room for the matches to **read** room to
54.1	691.25	**for** straws who **read** straws now who
62.5	691.33	**for** Christmas if **read** Christmas day if
70.14–71.11	692.4	**transfer** I saw to that **to 692.5 following** notice
74.12	692.8–9	**for** one deuying it **read** one denying it
83.8	692.17	**for** hes change **read** hes a change
126.5	693.23	**for** of a drink **read** of drink
127.10	693.24	**for** some liquor Id **read** some liqueur Id
131.13	693.28	**for** time we **read** time after we
136.12–137.6	693.31	**transfer** as if the world was coming to an end **to 693.34 following** Gibraltar
135.9	693.32–3	**for** punish when **read** punish us when
141.6–145.9	695.1–4	**transfer 695.1–4 to the beginning of p. 694 (the references given here for pp. 694–5 are to the lines as they stand on the pages of 1922; this error is not entered in the Historical Collation of 1984)**

143.8	695.2	**for** lamp yes because **read** lamp because
152.3	694.7	**for** us like **read** us or like
155.2	694.10	**for** pull it out **read** pull out
173.12–13	694.28	**for** neck on **read** neck it was on
177.2	694.31	**for** about every thing I **read** about everything I
180.8	694.34–5	**for** the insides I **read** the inside I
183.4,7	694.37	**for** had on a coolness with **read** had a coolness on with
190.15–16	695.11	**for** then wouldsend them **read** then would send them
195.8–14	695.16	**transfer** to her **to the beginning of the line, following** declaration
205.3	695.25	**for** me did **read** me and did
212.12	695.33	**for** falling one **read** falling out one
216.3	695.36	**for** her month water **read** her mouth water
225.11	696.8	**for** Poldy anyway whatever **read** Poldy anyhow whatever
228.5	696.10–11	**for** like that and **read** like then and
229.5–6	696.12	**for** postcard up up **read** postcard U p up
240.10	696.23	**for** tea of flypaper **read** tea off flypaper
261.18	697.6	**for** my mouth a **read** my month a
266.9	697.11	**for** street well and **read** street west and
309.4	698.17	**for** with sunray **read** with the sunray
327.11–328.2	698.35–6	**for** writing a letter every morning sometimes **read** writing every morning a letter sometimes

354.3–4,6	699.24	**for** then he wouldnt believe next **read** then hed never believe the next
368.11	700.1	**for** suppose there'll be **read** suppose therell be
386.3	700.19	**for** man Griffith is **read** man Griffiths is
387.16	700.21	**for** of politics **read** of their politics
395.4	700.28	**for** the old **read** the other old
407.3	701.3	**for** going around with **read** going round with
431.9	701.26	**for** it it was **read** it was
456.7	702.14	**for** it thin **read** it the thin
466.6	702.24	**for** paltry handerchiefs about **read** paltry handkerchiefs about
486.13	703.7–8	**for** thing around her **read** thing round her
492.1	703.13	**for** with the old **read** with that old
526.12–13	704.10	**for** trouble whats she there **read** trouble what shes there
544.11–559.11	704.34–705.12	**transfer** that disgusting [...] something there **to 704.28 following** cabbageleaf **and insert** about her **in 705.12 to precede** and that **so that the reconnected words read** asked him about her and that **(the references given here are to the lines as they stand on the pages of 1922)**
551.14	705.4	**for** eye or if **read** eye as if
553.4	705.5–6	**delete repeated** of those rotten places the night coming home with
564.8	704.33	**for** has the nymphs **read** has nymphs
598.10	706.7	**for** old sweet sonnnng the **read** old sweeeetsonnnng the

601.9	706.10	**for** lying around hes **read** lying about hes
605.15	706.14	**for** is the rain **read** is that rain
606.4–5	706.14	**for** lovely just **read** lovely and refreshing just
610.12	706.19	**delete** the mosquito nets and
613.14	706.22	**for** on what she **read** on it she
614.12–13	706.23	**for** a P C to **read** a p c to
615.13	706.24	**for** a very clean **read** a *very* clean
623.6,8	706.31–2	**for** love yes affly xxxxx **read** love yrs affly Hester xxxxx
627.1	706.35	**for** ear clothes **read** ear these clothes
642.14	707.13	**for** with lhe pillow **read** with the pillow
648.5–650.7	707.19	**following** change **insert** he was attractive to a girl in spite of his being a little bald intelligent looking disappointed and gay at the same time he was like Thomas in the shadow of Ashlydyat
659.3	707.27	**for** always shopifting anything **read** always shoplifting anything
660.1	707.28	**for** it this **read** it O this
661.6	707.29–30	**for** rolled up under **read** rolled under
667.2	707.35	**for** never come back **read** never came back
670.4,5	708.1	**for** the swell of the ship **read** the smell of ship
681.6	708.12	**for** directions of you **read** directions if you
683.10	708.14	**for** the codsul that **read** the consul that
685.4–5	708.16	**for** old reveille **read** old bugles for reveille
697.8	708.27	**for** I supposed he **read** I suppose he

718.14	709.11–12	**for** now whatever possessed **read** now what possessed
719.4–5	709.12	**for** write after **read** write from Canada after
722.12	709.15	**for** always good humour well **read** always goodhumoured well
727.1	709.19	**for** acute pneumonia well **read** acute neumonia well
728.4–5	709.20	**for** mine its **read** mine poor Nancy its
730.2,9	709.22,23	**for** bereavement symphathy [...] newphew with **read** bereavement symphathy [...] newphew with
736.7	709.28	**for** Madrid silly **read** Madrid stuff silly
739.6	709.31	**for** all around you **read** all round you
743.15–744.2	709.35–6	**for** with precipit precipitancy with **read** with precipat precip itancy with
764.11	710.19	**for** passing I **read** passing but I
773.3	710.27	**for** engaged for fun **read** engaged for for fun
774.7	710.28	**for** believed that **read** believed me that
781.4	710.34–5	**for** left may yes **read** left May yes
788.4	711.4	**for** open at the **read** open in the
801.9	711.17	**for** fear your never **read** fear you never
804.9	711.20	**for** somewhere yes because **read** somewhere because
807.4	711.22–3	**for** never get far **read** never go far
808.12–809.2	711.24	**for** there all the time so tender how **read** there so tender all the time how
811.8	711.27	**for** petticoat I **read** petticoat because I

812.3	711.27	**for** I tortured the **read** I tormented the
813.5	711.28	**for** hotel rrrsssst awokwokawok **read** hotel rrrsssstt awokwokawok
814.14	711.30	**for** that morning I **read** that moaning I
819.15	711.35	**for** went around to **read** went round to
831.7–8	712.9	**for** were finrom Benady **read** were in from Benady
836.2	712.13	**for** his peaked cap **read** his peak cap
840.14	712.18	**for** never tho ught that **read** never thought that
846.12	712.24	**for** mother whœver she **read** mother whoever she
848.11	712.26	**for** along Willis road **read** along Williss road
849.1	712.26–7	**for** to Europe point **read** to Europa point
856.5	712.34	**for** up windmill hill **read** up Windmill hill
863.7	713.4	**for** the handerchief under **read** the handkerchief under
869.14–15	713.10	**for** pearl must **read** pearl still it must
870.2–3	713.10	**for** pure 16 carat gold **read** pure 18 carrot gold
870.10–873.5	713.10	**following** very heavy **insert** but what could you get in a place like that the sandfrog shower from Africa and that derelict ship that came up the harbour Marie the Marie whatyoucallit no he hadnt a moustache that was Gardner yes
877.4	713.14	**for** sweet ssooooooong Ill **read** sweet sooooooooooong Ill
881.6	713.18–19	**for** Irish homenade beauties **read** Irish homemade beauties

882.11	713.19–20	**for** and publicasn I **read** and publicans I
907.14–15	714.7	**for** my sidep iano quietly **read** my side piano quietly
908.11	714.8	**for** more song **read** more tsong
925.4	714.24	**for** us Goodbye to **read** us goodbye to
930.10	714.30	**for** tea Findon **read** tea and Findon
946.11	715.8	**for** gave 5/ each **read** gave 5/– each
947.1	715.9	**for** pay and **read** pay it and
955.5	715.17	**for** the boatmen he **read** the boatman he
958.2	715.19	**for** me to pull **read** me pull
959.2	715.20–21	**for** through through the **read** through the
992.9	716.16	**for** in Lloyd's Weekly **read** in Lloyds Weekly
1006.6	716.29	**for** to skerrys academy **read** to Skerrys academy
1007.4	716.30	**for** all at **read** all 1s at
1013.17	716.36	**for** her it he **read** her if he
1020.13–1021.16	717.5–6	**transfer** and helping […] not him **to 717.7 following** fact
1021.12–13	717.6	**for** its meshed tell **read** its me shed tell
1040.6	717.24	**for** go in **read** go on in
1041.12	717.26	**for** pit at the pit at **read** pit at
1047.3	717.31	**for** me and **read** me yes and
1057.8	718.4	**for** are few **read** are a few
1063.1	718.9	**for** lost always **read** lost shes always

1082.3	718.28	**for** Mrs Flemming you **read** Mrs Fleming you
1085.12	718.31	**for** the window **read** the area window
1092.9	719.1	**for** us wonder **read** us I wonder
1105.13–14	719.14	**for** that afflicty ou of **read** that afflict you of
1110.15–16	719.18	**for** only tim ewe were **read** only time we were
1112.12	719.20	**for** him Drimmies **read** him in Drimmies
1124.11–16	719.32	**for** sheets the **read** sheets I just put on I suppose the
1162.10	720.31–2	**for** my compriment I **read** my compriments I
1179.9	721.10–11	**for** 4 or 5 **read** 4 and 5
1214.5	722.7	**for** it form Lord **read** it from Lord
1232.2	722.25	**for** hour wait **read** hour 1 wait
1290.3–7	724.8	**for** him and **read** him trotting off in his trowlers and
1295.2	724.12	**for** goodbye *sweet*heart **read** goodbye sweetheart *sweet*heart
1308.12–1309.12	724.25	**for** other of **read** other the first cry was enough for me I heard the deathwatch too ticking in the wall of
1318.3	724.33–4	**for** by laud then **read** by land then
1324.17	725.3	**for** like Byron **read** like Lord Byron
1354.5	725.32	**for** he looked with **read** he looks with
1360.12	726.1	**for** wishcard come out **read** wishcard comes out
1364.11	726.5	**for** faints nnder me **read** faints under me
1382.10–11	726.22	**for** swelling upon you **read** swelling up on you

1392.8	726.32	**for** for stupid **read** for their stupid
1412.19	727.15	**for** only to do **read** only do
1464.10	728.29	**for** father Vial plana of **read** father Vilaplana of
1465.9	728.29–30	**for** y O'Reilly in **read** y OReilly in
1504.10	729.31	**for** the in the longing **read** the longing
1508.12	729.35	**for** son più forte **read** son piu forte
1515.14	730.5	**for** it in **read** it out in
1519.13	730.9	**for** He wouldn't have **read** He wouldnt have
1523.8	730.13	**for** perhaps 30/ Ill **read** perhaps 30/– Ill
1543.13	730.33	**for** office the **read** office or the
1556.6	731.7	**for** of course a **read** of those a
1560.4	731.11	**for** with fields **read** with the fields
1595.3	732.9	**for** posadas glancing **read** posadas 2 glancing
1600.8	732.14	**for** and pink **read** and the pink

ALTERATIONS TO
1961

1: Telemachus

6.11	3.6–7	**for** called up coarsely: **read** called out coarsely:
24.9	3.26	**for** long low whistle **read** long slow whistle
53.10	4.19	**for** know, Dedalus; you **read** know, Dedalus, you
77.13	5.5–6	**for** a grey sweet **read** a great sweet
86.5	5.14	**for** his great searching **read** his grey searching
112.17	6.3	**for** and few **read** and a few
194.7	8.14	**for** and I went **read** and went
245.13	9.29	**for** harpstrings merging **read** harpstrings, merging
248.9	9.32	**for** slowly, shadowing **read** slowly, wholly, shadowing
249.5	9.33	**for** lay behind him, **read** lay beneath him,
255.5	9.40	**for** fans, tasselled dancecards, **read** fans, tasseled dancecards,
258.3	10.2–3	**for** of Turko the terrible and **read** of *Turko the Terrible* and
279.1	10.26	**for** No mother. **read** No, mother.
314.4	11.25–6	**for** briskly about the hearth to and fro, hiding **read** briskly to and fro about the hearth, hiding
316.5	11.27	**for** high barbicans: and **read** high barbacans: and

324.1	11.37	**new paragraph at** He howled
340.7–8	12.16	**for** said. There's **read** said thirstily. There's
349.1	12.25	**new paragraph at** He hacked
417.1–6	14.18–19	**insert paragraph** – Look at that now, she said.
428.16	14.32	**for** from west, **read** from the west,
441.3	15.6	**for** filled the **read** filled again the
444.8–10	15.10	**for** shilling and **read** shilling. That's a shilling and
490.4	16.16	**for** make money **read** make any money
515.11	17.3	**delete** Agenbite of inwit.
525.1	17.14	**begin new paragraph at** Resigned he
547.9	17.41	**for** made to **read** made out to
602.9	19.22–3	**for** brief birdlike cries. **read** brief birdsweet cries.
638.3	20.27	**for** am the servant **read** am a servant
666.6	21.19	**for** Britisher, Haines' voice **read** Britisher, Haines's voice

2: Nestor

1.1	24.1	**insert dialogue dash**
11.2	24.12	**for** I forgot the **read** I forget the
24.2	24.29	**for** the tissues of **read** the tissue of
32.11	24.39	**for** the waves. A **read** the water.

49.5	25.15	**for** death? They **read** death. They
59.2–3	25.27	**for** the history, sir? **read** the story, sir?
64.5	25.32	**for** *woful shepherd, weep* **read** *woful shepherds, weep*
87.8–9	26.17	**for** woven on **read** woven and woven on
108.1	27.1	**delete dialogue dash, delete indent**
163.3	28.22	**for** long shady strokes **read** long shaky strokes
186.5	29.7	**for** came stepping **read** came away stepping
190.11	29.12–13	**for** Stephen cried. **read** Stephen said.
213.13	29.38	**for** money, cowries **read** money cowries
242.13–14	30.30	**for** poet but **read** poet, yes, but
250.1	30.37	**new paragraph at** He tapped
266.9	31.15	**for** tartan fillibegs: Albert **read** tartan filibegs: Albert
269.10–12	31.19	**for** famine. Do **read** famine in '46. Do
306.1	32.21	**for** this important **read** this allimportant
309.3–310.3	32.24–5	**for** slush. Even money Fair rebel: ten **read** slush. *Fair Rebel! Fair Rebel!* Even money the favourite: ten
365.6	34.7	**for** fingers. Gabbles of **read** fingers. Gabble of
371.9	34.15	**for** knew the years **read** knew their years
380.14	34.27	**for** All history **read** All human history

3: Proteus

17.5	37.19	**for** the end of **read** the ends of
19.9	37.22–3	**for** money. Dominic Deasy **read** money. Dominie Deasy
23.7	37.26	**for** hear. A catalectic tetrameter **read** hear. Acatalectic tetrameter
49.3	38.14	**for** about him. Is **read** about Him. Is
55.3	38.22	**for** romped around him, **read** romped round him,
79.3–8	39.5	**after** nephew. **add** Sit down and take a walk.
96.13	39.24	**for** lawdeedaw air here; **read** lawdeedaw airs here;
100.7	39.28	**for** *aria de sortita.* **read** *aria di sortita.*
134.3–4	40.26	**for** *women!* What **read** *women! naked women!* What
141.4	40.34	**for** epiphanies on **read** epiphanies written on
151.2–152.3	41.3	**for** breath. He **read** breath, a pocket of seaweed smouldered in seafire under a midden of man's ashes. He
167.15	41.21–2	**for** M. Leo Taxil. **read** M. Léo Taxil.
199.1	42.15	**for** Mother dying **read** Nother dying
212.11	42.31	**for** her hands. In **read** her hand. In
227.8–228.4	43.8	**for** now. To **read** now, AE, pimander, good shepherd of me. To
242.10	43.26	**for** veil orangeblossoms, **read** veil, orangeblossoms,
272.1	44.17	**for** the barbicans the **read** the barbacans the

289.3	44.36	**for** And there, the **read** And these, the
298.5	45.8	**for** safe among the **read** safe mong the
326.16	45.41	**for** of sands quickly **read** of sand quickly
349.9	46.28	**for** it, sniffing rapidly **read** it, sniffling rapidly
358.6	46.38	**for** lifting his **read** lifting again his
360.2	46.40	**for** scattered sand: **read** scattered the sand:
378.5	47.19–20	**for** in rogue's rum **read** in rogues' rum
402.1	48.8	**for** her womb. Oomb, **read** her moomb. Oomb,
404.1	48.10	**for** roaring wayawayawayawayawayaway. Paper. **read** roaring wayawayawayawayawayaway. Paper.
405.6	48.12	**for** for hospitality **read** for the hospitality
440.7	49.10–11	**for** *bona.* Alo! *Bonjour,* **read** *bona.* Hlo! *Bonjour,*
451.9–12	49.23	**for** name. He **read** name. His arm: Cranly's arm. He
473.5–11	50.7–8	**for** bobbing landward, a pace a pace a porpoise. **read** bobbing a pace a pace a porpoise landward.
474.5	50.9	**for** quick. Sunk **read** quick. Pull. Sunk
487.12	50.26	**for** and his my sandal **read** and hismy sandal

4: Calypso

3.6	55.3–4	**for** fried hencod's roes. **read** fried hencods' roes.

15.1	55.15	**begin new paragraph at** The cat
27.11–28.10	55.31, 36–7	**transfer** Cruel. Her nature. Curious mice never squeal. Seem to like it. **from 55.36–7 to 55.31 following** Vindictive too. **and delete new paragraph**
53.1	56.21	**for** – I am going **read** – I'm going
87.10	57.19	**for** moustaches leaning **read** moustaches, leaning
90.1	57.22	**for** crosslegged smoking **read** crosslegged, smoking
91.6	57.24	**for** sherbet. Wander along **read** sherbet. Dander along
93.2	57.26	**for** mosques along the **read** mosques among the
95.2	57.28	**for** watches from **read** watches me from
97.13	57.31	**for** of these instruments **read** of those instruments
136.2	58.33	**for** Joseph's, National **read** Joseph's National
141.5	58.39	**for** white. Fifty multiplied **read** white. Fifteen multiplied
142.1	58.40	**for** mind unsolved: **read** mind, unsolved:
144.4	59.1–2	**for** spicy pig's blood. **read** spicy pigs' blood.
147.7	59.5	**for** hand. Chapped: **read** hand? Chapped:
154.3–5	59.15	**for** took up a page from **read** took a page up from
158.2–3	59.19	**for** nearer, the **read** nearer, the title, the
192.2	60.17	**for** Netaim: planter's company. **read** Netaim: planters' company.

192.6	60.17	**for** purchase vast sandy **read** purchase waste sandy
195.2	60.20	**for** pay eight marks **read** pay eighty marks
218.7–8	61.7	**for** sun wholly slowly wholly. **read** sun slowly, wholly.
220.12	61.10–11	**for** wind would lift **read** wind could lift
224.10	61.15–16	**for** a noggin bottle **read** a naggin bottle
243.11	61.35	**for** He stopped and **read** He stooped and
244.6	61.36	**for** His quick heart **read** His quickened heart
274.1	62.26	**for** kettle and crushed **read** kettle, crushed
284.12	62.39	**for** No wait. **read** No, wait.
314.1	63.31	**for** – *La ci* **read** – *Là ci*
338.3	64.16	**for** leaned downwards and **read** leaned downward and
344.8	64.23	**for** mocking eye. The **read** mocking eyes. The
351.11	64.32	**for** they metempsychosis. That **read** they metamspychosis. That
359.9	64.40	**for** watching its flow **read** watching it flow
368.1	65.10	**for** An example. **read** An example?
409.13–14	66.16	**for** respects. Must **read** respects. I must
445.1	67.14	**for** Reading lying **read** Reading, lying
447.3	67.16	**for** qualm regret, **read** qualm, regret,
450.4	67.19	**for** kissing kissed. **read** kissing, kissed.
489.1	68.24	**for** Brown brilliantined hair **read** Brown brillantined hair

519.3–4	69.19	**for** proverb which? **read** proverb. Which?
524.10–11	69.25–6	**delete new paragraph and run on** Rubbing smartly **following** her boot.
525.5	69.26	**for** her stocking calf. **read** her stockinged calf.
529.14	69.32	**for** good smell **read** good rich smell
549.10	70.15	**for** air, third. **read** air. A third.

5 : Lotus Eaters

2.7	71.2–3	**for** linseed crusher's, the **read** linseed crusher, the
11.12	71.14	**for** the undertaker's. At **read** the undertaker. At
12.10	71.15	**for** bagged that job **read** bagged the job
13.7	71.16	**for** shut. Corney. Met **read** shut. Corny. Met
27.12–28.12	71.33–4	**for** over again: **read** over his brow and hair. Then he put on his hat again, relieved: and read again:
32.3	71.37–8	**for** lobbing around in **read** lobbing about in
38.1–2	72.3	**for** Ah, in **read** Ah yes, in
41.1–2	72.6	**for** the. Or **read** the what? Or
41.10	72.7	**for** equal of the **read** equal to the
61.4	72.29	**for** thanked and **read** thanked her and
111.3	74.6	**for** his veiled eyelids **read** his vailed eyelids
118.8	74.14–15	**for** he fostering over **read** he foostering over
134.2	74.31	**for** hallway. Monday **read** hallway Monday

156.6	75.16	**for** man. Cat **read** man. Letter. Cat
161.2	75.22	**for** *Comes lo-ve's old ...* **read** *Comes lo-ove's old ...*
162.14	75.24	**for** thoughtfully. *Sweet song.* **read** thoughtfully. *Sweeeet song.*
195.1	76.23	**for** Mrs Bandman Palmer. **read** Mrs Bandmann Palmer.
195.7–9	76.24	**for** in that again. **read** again in that.
197.10	76.26	**for** talk about Kate **read** talk of Kate
203.1	76.33	**delete dialogue dash**
208.13	76.39	**for** was the best **read** was best
227.1	77.17	**for** *La ci* **read** *Là ci*
235.9	77.26–7	**for** his mantel not **read** his mantle not
253.5	78.6	**for** not write. O **read** not wrote. O
269.2	78.25	**for** she write it **read** she wrote it
281.2	78.38	**for** *0, Mary lost* **read** *O, Mairy lost*
323.13–326.2	80.7–9	**transfer** Prayers for the conversion of Gladstone they had too when he was almost unconscious. The protestants the same. Convert Dr. William J. Walsh D.D. to the true religion. **to 80.4 following** African mission.
325.3	80.8	**for** protestants the **read** protestants are the
352.8–9	80.37	**for** corpse why **read** corpse. Why
364.7	81.10–11	**for** a big spreeish **read** a bit spreeish
423.1	82.40	**for** mass? Gloria and **read** mass? Glorious and

455.5–456.1	83.33–4	**transfer** Annoyed if you don't. Why didn't you tell me before. **to 83.36 following** the moon.
478.7	84.21	**for** Doctor whack. He **read** Doctor Whack. He
498.14	85.2	**for** Leopold yes. **read** Leopold, yes.
501.11–13	85.5	**transfer** Pure curd soap. **to 85.6 following** soaps have. **and read** That orangeflower water is so fresh.
564.8	86.33	**for** dearer than them **read** dearer thaaan them

6: Hades

24.9	87.28	**for** front turning: **read** front, turning:
49.9	88.15	**for** *fidus Achates?* **read** *fidus Achates!*
123.7	90.17–18	**for** with illness compared. **read** with illnesses compared.
185.2	92.5	**for** Mrs Bandman Palmer **read** Mrs Bandmann Palmer
220.1	93.5	**delete dialogue dash and run on to previous paragraph**
240.10	93.28	**for** A thrust. A **read** A thrush. A
241.3	93.29	**for** that expressed that. **read** that expresses that.
281.2	94.36	**for** For God's sake! **read** For God' sake!
297.1	95.14	**for** – And then **read** – Ah then
428.6	98.39	**for** up drowning **read** up, drowning
486.5	100.22	**for** of Prospects rippled **read** of Prospect rippled

554.7	102.19	**for** alone under **read** alone, under
576.1	103.4	**for** and the **read** and at the
626.1	104.22	**for** little sparrow's breasts. **read** little sparrows' breasts.
716.6	107.4	**for** two keys **read** two long keys
749.1	108.3	**for** death … Shades **read** death. Shades
760.11	108.17	**for** of frilled beefsteaks **read** of grilled beefsteaks
822.6	110.7–8	**for** coffin. Enbalming in **read** coffin. Embalming in
862.12	111.13	**for** Mamma poor **read** Mamma, poor
965.5	114.5	**for** kraark awfullygladaseeragain hellohello **read** kraark awfullygladaseeagain hellohello
966.2–3	114.5–6	**for** hellohello amarawf kopthsth. Remind **read** hellohello amawf krpthsth. Remind
1033.8	115.41	**for** this morning. **read** this morning!

7: Aeolus

25.3	116.27	**for** is Red **read** is, Red
45.5	117.18	**for** passed stately up **read** passed statelily up
77.1–79.3	118.17–19	**transfer** WITH UNFEIGNED REGRET IT IS WE ANNOUNCE THE DISSOLUTION OF A MOST RESPECTED DUBLIN BURGESS **to 118.21 following** Thumping thump. **and begin 118.21** This morning **with a paragraph indent**

92.1   119.1–2   **for** of Tinnachinch. To **read** of Tinnahinch.
                              To

97.4   119.8   **for** note M.A.P. **read** note. M.A.P.

123.6   119.39   **for** cutting a while and **read** cutting awhile
                              and

128.7–13   120.1   **transfer** He doesn't hear it. Nannan. Iron
                              nerves. **to 120.5 following** they make.

140.4–5   120.19   **for** scarred-woodwork. **read** scarred
                              woodwork.

174.10   121.22–3   **for** jogged forwards its **read** jogged forward its

219.3   122.34   **for** out perhaps? Better **read** out perhaps.
                              Better

228.10   123.9   **for** buttoned into **read** buttoned, into

231.6–7   123.11   **for** see before dressing. **read** see: before:
                              dressing.

245.7–10   123.26   **transfer** *fanned by gentlest zephyrs* **to 123.28**
                              following *mossy banks,* **and add comma**
                              after *zephyrs*

313.6   125.25   **for** for God's sake, **read** for God' sake,

326.1–3   126.1   **transfer** HIS NATIVE DORIC **to 126.2–3**
                              following forgot Hamlet.

369.2   127.12   **for** A Perfect cretic! **read** A perfect cretic!

370.3   127.13   **for** HARP EOLIAN **read** HARP EOLIAN!

403.13   128.20   **for** Pat Farrel shoved **read** Pat Farrell shoved

442.1   129.29   **for** – Show! Where? **read** – Show. Where?

521.13   132.11   **for** short taken. **read** short taken?

545.8   133.1   **for** it? J.J. **read** it, J.J.

549.10   133.6   **for** began. Hungarian **read** began. A
                              Hungarian

591.4	134.19	**for** *of Castille.* See **read** *of Castile.* See
604.1–2	135.1	**transfer** OMNIUM GATHERUM **to 135.2–3 following** Stephen said.
614.1, 4	135.13	**for** YOU CAN DO IT! **read** "YOU CAN DO IT!"
622.1	135.23	**for** Father Son **read** Father, Son
694.1	137.35	**new paragraph at** He flung
719.1–2	138.25	**for** .....*mentrechè il* **read** .....*mentreche il*
722.7–8	138.28–9	**for** *rimirar fe piu ardenti.* **read** *rimirar fè più ardenti.*
769.10	140.14	**for** *and prophecy* **read** *and of prophecy*
769.12	140.14	**for** *which if* **read** *which, if*
834.10	142.12–13	**for** their smoke ascending **read** their smokes ascending
918.1	144.34	**for** – Yes, the **read** – Yes? the
926.2–4	145.6	**for** Off Blackpitts. **read** Off Blackpitts, Stephen said.
962.1–3	146.10	**transfer** RETURN OF BLOOM **to 146.11–12 following** see them.
963.1	146.12	**delete dialogue dash**
998.10–999.1	147.19	**transfer** You must take the will for the deed. **to follow** Sorry, Jack.
1003.6	147.24	**for** the beard was **read** the bread was
1025.6	148.17	**for** it one **read** it, one
1049.5	149.15	**for** rattled, lolled, horsedrawn, **read** rattled, rolled, horsedrawn,

8: Lestrygonians

13.1	151.15	**for** burntoffering, druid's altars. **read** burntoffering, druids' altars.
79.5–9	153.13	**for** on fishy flesh they have to, all **read** on fish, fishy flesh they have, all
95.15	153.31	**for** All kind of **read** All kinds of
121.9	154.18–19	**for** at storing away **read** at stowing away
168.7	155.33	**for** glove, shoulder and **read** glove, shoulders and
244.2	157.36–7	**for** medicinebottle. Pastile that **read** medicinebottle. Pastille that
247.11	157.41	**for** him wide **read** him, wide
301.8	159.22	**for** question. Mrs **read** question? Mrs
348.1	160.36	**for** car: wishwish. Stonewall **read** car: wishswish. Stonewall
349.15	160.38	**for** O yes? Mrs **read** O yes! Mrs
359.12–15	161.8	**for** dairy. Eating **read** dairy. Y.M.C.A. Eating
360.10–11	161.8–9	**for** minute. Still **read** minute. And still
425.7	162.42	**for** street. Luck I **read** street. Lucky I
455.2	163.34	**for** Ah, get along with **read** Ah, gelong with
472.10	164.12–13	**for** home. Shove us **read** home. Show us
490.6	164.33	**for** Slaves. Chinese **read** Slaves Chinese
500.1,5	165.2	**for** ware in Walter Sexton's window opposite by **read** ware opposite in Walter Sexton's window by

584.11–12	167.17	**for** moon, she **read** moon out, she
594.6	167.28	**for** relief, his **read** relief his
609.2–3	168.3	**for** twentythree when **read** twentythree. When
615.2	168.11	**for** prints, silk, dames and **read** prints, silkdames and
722.5	171.7	**for** to animal **read** to the animal
737.1–2	171.25	**for** – Hellow, Bloom! Nosey **read** – Hello, Bloom, Nosey
742.5	171.31	**for** descendants mustered and **read** descendants musterred and
755.9	172.5–6	**for** itself. Mighty cheese. **read** itself. Mity cheese.
789.9	172.42	**for** mustard hauched on **read** mustard hanched on
829.3	174.1	**for** sport now. **read** sport going now.
843.3	174.17	**for** champing standing, **read** champing, standing,
847.4	174.22	**for** like. Dog's cold **read** like. Dogs' cold
864.1	174.42	**for** oysters? Unsightly **read** oysters. Unsightly
923.6	176.29	**for** speaking, I **read** speaking. I
998.9	178.29–30	**for** for God's sake? **read** for God' sake?
1058.11–1059.10	180.14	**for** Presscott's ad. **read** Prescott's dyeworks van over there. If I got Billy Prescott's ad.
1084.3	180.41	**for** his brilliantined hair **read** his brillantined hair

1109.3–12	181.27	**for** Weight. Would **read** Weight or size of it, something blacker than the dark. Wonder would
1110.8	181.28	**for** removed? Feel **read** removed. Feel
1122.2–5	181.41	**for** together. Each **read** together. Each street different smell. Each
1128.1	182.6	**for** voice temperature **read** voice, temperature
1128.8	182.7	**for** with fingers **read** with his fingers
1164.6	183.7	**for** Yes Handel. **read** Yes, Handel.

9: Scylla and Charybdis

16.4	184.18	**for** la Palisse, Stephen **read** la Palice, Stephen
52.3	185.18	**for** our mind into **read** our minds into
108.5	187.3	**for** song, France **read** song. France
132.11	187.30	**for** one, Our **read** one. Our
174.1	189.1	**delete dialogue dash**
238.7	190.33	**for** the caudlectures saved **read** the caudlelectures saved
239.7	190.34	**for** their noggin of **read** their naggin of
263.11	191.22	**for** gladly brightly. **read** gladly, brightly.
321.1	193.2	**for** Good ild **read** God ild
322.1	193.3	**delete dialogue dash**
426.1	195.38	**for** *d'être grand* ... **read** *d'être grandp* ...
456.13–457.1	196.27	**for** first (ryefield, **read** first (a ryefield,

464.3	196.36	**for** A life fate **read** A like fate
485.11	197.19–20	**for** came forwards then **read** came forward then
492.5–6	197.28	**for** Photius, pseudomalachi, Johann **read** Photius, pseudo Malachi, Johann
494.1	197.30	**for** sent himself, Agenbuyer, **read** sent Himself, Agenbuyer,
500.1–4	197.34	**transfer musical notation and** *Glo– o-ri-a in ex-cel-sis De-o.* **to 198.3–4 following** dead already.
501.3	198.4	**for** lifts hands. **read** lifts his hands.
503.10	198.7	**for** discussion, Mr **read** discussion. Mr
610.2	201.4	**for** museum when I **read** museum where I
630.2	201.28	**for** The gombeen woman Eliza **read** The gombeenwoman Eliza
631.8	201.30	**for** between conjugal love **read** between conjugial love
638.2–3	201.37	**for** lakin, Mistress Fitten, mount **read** lakin, mistress Fitton, mount
703.1	203.27–8	**insert** Leftherhis **on a new line following** Secondbest
758.2	205.8	**for** otherwise carroty Bess, **read** otherwise carrotty Bess,
760.4	205.11	**for** the depth of **read** the depths of
794.2	206.8	**for** Which Will? gagged **read** Which will? gagged
809.3	206.25–6	**for** Venus had twisted **read** Venus has twisted
854.7	207.40	**for** The sun unborn **read** The son unborn **(corrected in some copies of 1961)**

860.3	208.5	**for** I father? **read** I a father?
870.8	208.17	**for** born for **read** born, for
939.4	210.19	**for** skies. *Autontimerumenos. Bous* **read** skies. *Autontimorumenos. Bous.*
941.8	210.21–2	**for** *non amar S.D.* **read** *non amare S.D.*
954.10	210.38	**for** Lapwing he. **read** Lapwing be.
955.2	210.39	**for** Mr Best's eagerquietly **read** Mr Best eagerquietly
959.3	211.1	**for** that marries **read** that always marries
1008.7–8	212.16–17	**for** Maynooth: an **read** Maynooth: – an
1014.7–8	212.24	**for** *Measure,* and **read** *Measure* – and
1105.5	215.4	**for** Irish nights' entertainment. **read** Irish nights entertainment
1128.2	215.30	**for** He sputtered to **read** He spluttered to
1132.2	215.34	**for** the public sweat **read** the pubic sweat
1140.8	216.1	**for** forgot … he … **read** forgot … eh …
1148.4	216.9	**for** *filibustering fillibeg* **read** *filibustering filibeg*

10: Wandering Rocks

1.8–9	219.1	**for** S.J., RESET **read** S.J. RESET
17.1	219.20	**for** leaves and **read** leaves: and
30.6–8	219.35	**for** hat, as **read** hat and smiled, as
49.7	220.16	**for** and laughed. **read** and laughed:
63.7	220.32	**for** she smiled. And **read** she sailed. And

69.11	220.39	**for** T. R. Green B. A. **read** T. R. Greene B. A.
100.9	221.32	**for** red, lying neatly **read** red, lie neatly
101.1	221.34	**no new paragraph at** Moored under
105.8	221.39	**for** bogs where men **read** bogs whence men
125.1	222.20	**new paragraph at** A tiny
141.7	222.41	**for** Stratton grinned with **read** Stratton grimaced with
144.6	223.2	**for** sermon of Saint **read** sermon on Saint
172.3	223.37	**for** for men's race **read** for man's race
183.3–5	224.7–8	**for** homely and just **read** just and homely
197.1	224.22–3	**new paragraph with dialogue dash at** *Principium verborum*
205.1	224.31	**new paragraph with dialogue dash at** *Principes persecuti*
239.12	225.28	**for** thanks and glanced **read** thanks, glanced
316.2	227.29	**for** hawker's car. **read** hawker's cart.
341.1	228.17	**for** gripping frankly the **read** gripping the
341.4	228.18	**for** handrests. Pale faces. Men's **read** handrests. Palefaces. Men's
345.14	228.23	**for** *bestia. É peccato.* **read** *bestia. È peccato.*
383.2	229.27	**for** way she is holding **read** way she's holding
523.3	233.30	**for** what he is buying, **read** what he's buying,
530.9	233.39	**for** about comet's tails **read** about comets' tails
547.13	234.17	**for** and curaçao to **read** and curacoa to

604.9	236.2	**for** Listen: The **read** Listen: the
612.7	236.13–14	**for** *her déshabillé.* **read** *her deshabille.*
615.1	236.17	**new paragraph at** *The beautiful*
620.1	236.23	**for** yielded amid **read** yielded amply amid
623.2	236.26–7	**for** Press! Crushed! Sulphur **read** Press! Chrished! Sulphur
645.3	237.10	**for** Dedalus, listening by **read** Dedalus, loitering by
658.11	237.26	**for** upon shoulders? Melancholy **read** upon shoulder? Melancholy
698.7	238.33	**for** Look, that's all **read** Look, there's all
718.9	239.14–15	**for** Kernan pleased **read** Kernan, pleased
719.9	239.15–16	**for** Robertson boldly **read** Robertson, boldly
723.3	239.19	**for** weather we are having **read** weather we're having
731.2	239.29	**for** now you are talking **read** now you're talking
757.11	240.20	**for** that Lambert's **read** that Ned Lambert's
767.1–768.3	240.29–30	**insert paragraph** Bad times those were. Well, well. Over and done with. Great topers too. Fourbottle men. **following** her noddy.
781.6	241.2	**no new paragraph at** Times of
819.10	242.9	**for** sanded umbrella, **read** sanded tired umbrella,
833.8	242.25	**for** in light loincloths **read** in tight loincloths
854.6	243.5	**for** here, Stephen. **read** here, Stephen?
900.1	244.17	**for** – There he **read** – Here he

920.1	244.40–41	**for** murmuring, glasseyed, strode **read** murmuring, glassyeyed, strode
984.2–4	246.33	*la Maison Claire* **in roman, not italic**
1012.1	247.22–3	**for** language, of **read** language, language of
1044.2	248.15	**for** his panama to **read** his Panama to
1051.11	248.25	**no new paragraph at** An instant
1109.6	250.8	**for** Wilde's he **read** Wilde's house he
1123.5	250.22	**for** and half **read** and a half
1135.1–2	250.36	**for** sovereigns, God, that'd **read** sovereigns. Gob, that'd
1173.2	251.41	**for** he is in **read** he's in
1218.10	253.15	**for** Dudley on **read** Dudley fixed on
1220.8	253.17	**for** charming *soubrette*, great **read** charming soubrette, great
1242.13	254.2	**no new paragraph at** Blazes Boylan
1250.3	254.11	**for** the *cortège*: **read** the cortège:
1258.1	254.19	**delete paragraph indent**
1262.10–11	254.24	**for** Mr E.M.Solomons **read** Mr M.E.Solomons

11: Sirens

1.7	256.1	**for** HOOFIRONS, STEELYRINING IMPER- **read** HOOFIRONS, STEELYRINGING IMPER-
2.1	256.1–2	**new segment at** Imperthnthn thnthnthn.
4.1	256.3–4	**new segment at** Horrid! And

8.11	256.8	**for** of Castille. **read** of Castile.
31.2	256.33	**for** A moonlight nightcall: **read** A moonlit nightcall:
54.3	257.15	**for** rose Castille of **read** rose Castile of
96.2	258.20	**for** Your *beau,* is **read** Your beau, is
115.2	258.41	**for** Miss Bronze unbloused **read** Miss bronze unbloused
127.8–9	259.13	**for** for mercy'sake! **read** for mercy' sake!
145.2	259.32	**for** a shout in **read** a snout in
175.1	260.25	**for** each other to **read** each each to
230.12	262.2	**for** Blue Bloom is **read** Blue bloom is
740.1	264.27	**for** – *Co-me, thou* **read** – *Co-ome, thou*
741.1	264.28	**for** – *Co-me thou* **read** – *Co-ome thou*
259.4	262.33	**for** famous fighter, laid **read** famous father, laid
295.6	263.32	**for** paper on reserve **read** paper one reserve
299.5	263.37	**for** mass. Tanks awfully **read** mass. Thanks awfully
306.1	264.4	**for** – Two pence, sir, **read** – Twopence, sir,
308.1	264.6	**insert dialogue dash**
329.9, 331.9	264.28,30	**for** of Castille. **read** of Castile.
343.9	265.2	**for** aloft saluting. **read** aloft, saluting.
405.5–7	266.25	**for** *Sonnezlacloche!* **read** *Sonnez la cloche!*
414.5	266.36	**for** smackable woman's **read** smackable a woman's

420.9	267.2–3	**for** drops. He spellbound **read** drops. His spellbound
444.8	267.27	**for** orders, Power **read** orders. Power
449.6	267.33	**for** Ben Dollar called. **read** Ben Dollard called.
452.6	267.38	**for** Plumped stopped **read** Plumped, stopped
498.2	269.9	**for** Jingle haunted down **read** Jingle jaunted down
575.3–4	271.12	**for** the 'cello, **read** the cello,
580.4–5	271.18	**for** Lovely gold **read** Lovely. Gold
594.2	271.33	**for** *tutt amor:* **read** *tutt'amor:*
608.1	272.6	**new paragraph at** Steak, kidney,
610.9	272.9–10	**for** said: *Sonnambula.* He **read** said: *Sonambula.* He
611.9	272.10–11	**for** Ah, that M'Guckin! **read** Ah, what M'Guckin!
631.1	272.34	**for** murmured all. **read** murmured: all.
675.8	273.41	**for** strings of reeds **read** strings or reeds
687.2–3	274.13	**for** feet when **read** feet. When
691.7	274.18	**for** Or? Phila of **read** Or? Phial of
709.2	274.39–40	**for** joygush, tupthrop. Now! **read** joygush, tupthrob. Now!
712.5	275.2	**for** of hope. **read** of hopk.
718.12	275.9	**for** waiting, to **read** waiting to
740.1	275.35	**for** – *Co-me, thou* **read** – *Co-ome, thou*
741.1	275.36	**for** – *Co-me thou* **read** – *Co-ome thou*

748.9	276.3	**for** the ethereal bosom, **read** the etherial bosom,
770.2	276.28	**for** two tankards **read** two more tankards
791.1	277.11	**for** The nights Si **read** The night Si
796.10	277.16–17	**for** It buzzed, it **read** It buzz, it
824.9	278.9	**for** catgut fine. It **read** catgut line. It
835.5	278.22	**for** the ethereal. But **read** the etherial. But
840.13	278.28	**for** sacks over **read** sacks, over
844.10–846.5	278.32–4	**transfer** *Blumenlied* I bought for her. The name. Playing it slow, a girl, night I came home, the girl. Door of the stables near Cecilia street. **to 278.35 following** I mean.
889.2	280.4	**for** know now. In **read** know how. In
904.12	280.25	**for** charms Shakespeare **read** charms. Shakespeare
945.12–13	281.29–30	**for** blood is it. Souse **read** blood it is. Souse
973.1–2	282.20	**for** silk. When **read** silk. Tongue when
975.3	282.22	**for** in *qui est* **read** in *quis est*
998.5	283.6	**for** talons gripped the **read** talons griped the
1011.3–4	283.21	**for** voice barreltone. **read** voice base barreltone.
1049.8	284.25	**for** music? Way **read** music. Way
1066.4	285.4	**for** last my **read** last of my
1101.12 1102.12	286.5–7	**for** martyrs. For all things dying, want to, dying to, die. For that all things born. **read** martyrs that want to, dying to, die. For all things dying, for all things born.

1109.9	286.14	**for** rose! Castille. The **read** rose! Castile. The
1110.1	286.15	**new paragraph at** Ha. Lidwell.
1125.2	286.32–3	**for** Farrell, Waaaaaaalk. **read** Farrell. Waaaaaaalk.
1154.2	287.21	**for** Big Benaden Dollard. **read** Big Benaben Dollard.
1178.7,9	288.8	**for** summer Dollard left Bloom felt **read** summer dollard left bloom felt
1191.3	288.22	**for** he stunts himself **read** he stuns himself
1202.5	288.35	**for** little pippy wind. **read** little pipy wind.
1204.1	288.37	**insert dialogue dash**
1207.3	288.40	**for** the by there's **read** the bye there's
1250.12	290.5	**for** brown mackin. O, **read** brown macin. O,
1257.10–12	290.13–14	**for** stroke. That appointment **read** stroke, that. Appointment
1271.7	290.29	**for** of Castille. First **read** of Castile. First

12: Cyclops

13.6	292.15	**for** There is a **read** There's a
19.1	292.22	**for** – Circumcised! says **read** – Circumcised? says
29.3–4	292.33	**for** *so will I, for* **read** *so I will, for*
34.2–7	292.38	**for** parade, Wood **read** parade in the city of Dublin, Wood
38.9–11	293.1	**for** shillings per **read** shillings and no pence per

55.6	293.20	**for** he's in **read** he's out in
73.4–5	294.1	**for** flounder, the **read** flounder, the pollock, the
83.9	294.13	**for** from Elbana to **read** from Eblana to
100.1	294.33	**delete dialogue dash**
111.1	295.3	**for** of Lush and **read** of Lusk and
174.5	296.32	**for** which dangled at **read** which jangled at
185.7	297.3–4	**for** of Castille, the **read** of Castile, the
189.4	297.8	**for** Michelangelo, Hayes, **read** Michelangelo Hayes
234.5	298.18	**for** of Davie Dimsey, **read** of David Dimsey,
237.1	298.21	**for** son? How's **read** son! How's
273.1	299.23	**insert dialogue dash**
281.5	299.31	**for** the foaming ebon **read** the foamy ebon
303.12	300.17	**for** hanging. I'll **read** hanging, I'll
311.9	300.25	**for** be bit **read** be a bit
311.13	300.25	**for** dust. Bob's **read** dust Bob's
327.10	301.1	**for** and Willie Murray **read** and Willy Murray
331.4	301.5	**for** Alf. He is no **read** Alf. He's no
372.1	302.12	**no new paragraph at** Assurances were
398.3	303.2	**for** him to go **read** him go
399.3	303.3–4	**for** daughter. Mother **read** daughter, Mother
399.10	303.4	**for** street that **read** street, that

409.8–11	303.14	**transfer** he won't eat you, **to the end of the line, and read** citizen. He won't eat you.
415.2	303.20	**insert dialogue dash**
420.11	303.24	**for** *of February* 1900 **read** *of Febuary* 1900
429.1	303.34	**for** *five ginnese.* **read** *five ginnees.*
436.2	304.2	**for** and couldn't **read** and he couldn't
471.6	304.42–305.1	**for** approved traditions of **read** approved tradition of
473.2–10	305.3	**for** centres, causing the pores **read** centres of the genital apparatus, thereby causing the elastic pores
477.1	305.7	**for** been dominated by **read** been denominated by
485.6	305.17	**for** brute sniffling and **read** brute sniffing and
488.8	305.21	**for** with him: **read** with his:
489.12	305.23	**for the first** Give us the **read** Give the
495.11	305.29	**for** a Jacob's tin **read** a Jacobs' tin
562.1	307.26	**for** Karamelopulos. Ali **read** Karamelopulos, Ali
565.9–566.5	307.30–32	**for** Goosepond Prhklstr Kratchinabritchisitch, Herr Hurhausdirektorpräsident Hans **read** Goosepond Přhklštř Kratchinabritchisitch, Borus Hupinkoff, Herr Hurhausdirektorpresident Hans
573.1	307.38–9	**for** among F.O.T.E.I. **read** among the F.O.T.E.I.
612.4	308.42–309.1	**for** supplication. Hard by **read** supplication. Hand by

635.1	309.27–8	**for** indigent roomkeeper's association **read** indigent roomkeepers' association
643.12	309.38	**for** would cherish **read** would ever cherish
668.10	310.26	**for** shamrock excitement **read** shamrock the excitement
679.4	310.39	**for** the citizens begins **read** The citizen begins
682.15	311.1	**for** off Joe **read** off of Joe
701.8	311.22	**for** citizen, sneering. **read** citizen, jeering.
702.12	311.23	**for** a lampost. **read** a lamppost.
715.5–6	311.37–8	**for** red wolfdog setter formerly **read** red setter wolfdog formerly
729.6	312.12	**for** of Donald MacConsidine **read** of Donal MacConsidine
732.14	312.16–17	**for** believe our **read** believe that our
770.9	313.15–16	**for** about the mortgagor **read** about mortgagor
807.8	314.18	**for** and snugging. And **read** and smugging. And
869.3	316.8	**for** Orelli (Montenotte. **read** Orelli O'Reilly (Montenotte.
888.7	316.29	**for** known. Do you **read** known. Did you
889.7	316.31	**for** Irish sport and **read** Irish sports and
889.13	316.32	**for** of the lawn **read** of lawn
891.9	316.34	**for** all of that. **read** all to that.
902.1	317.4	**for** of this noble **read** of the noble
911.7	317.15	**for** and power handed **read** and prowess handed

922.10	317.28–9	**for** greatly enchanced his **read** greatly enhanced his
924.3	317.30	**for** audience amongst which **read** audience among which
945.12	318.14	**for** training of the **read** training the
947.16	318.16	**for** run the **read** run up the
958.6	318.27	**for** wind. Queensberry **read** wind, Queensberry
1002.10	319.35–6	**for** you Caddereesh. **read** you Caddareesh.
1008.11	319.42	**for** the O'Molloys, a **read** the O'Molloy's, a
1029.4	320.23	**for** Gob, ye'll come **read** Gob, he'll come
1029.12	320.24	**for** of these days, **read** of those days,
1060.10, 1061.1	321.16–17	**for** Bloom explained he meant, on **read** Bloom explaining he meant on
1066.12	321.24	**for** The signor Brini **read** The signior Brini
1107.2	322.29	**for** And a wife **read** And the wife
1117.5	322.41	**for** the claims of **read** the claim of
1120.1	323.2–3	**for** vintner, deceased versus **read** vintner, deceased, versus
1131.13	323.17	**for** true delivrance make **read** true deliverance make
1134.4	323.20	**for** the books. And **read** the book. And
1143.13	323.32	**for** Joe telling **read** Joe, telling
1157.2–3	324.4	**for** them. The **read** them in. The
1163.8	324.11	**for** citizen, that's what's the **read** citizen, that was the

1248.3	326.21	**for** world! Where **read** world. Where
1326.2	328.33	**for** up on a **read** up in a
1387.3–4	330.22	**for** an *Entente cordiale* now **read** an entente cordial now
1388.8	330.24	**for** always were? **read** always were.
1408.6	331.6–7	**for** their lordship's decision. **read** their lordships' decision.
1426.6	331.26	**for** had a laugh **read** had the laugh
1465.1	332.29	**for** – Shove us **read** – Show us
1472.1	332.38	**for** auction off in **read** auction in
1472.7	332.38–9	**for** or cattles. **read** or cattle.
1490.12	333.23	**for** your neighbours. **read** your neighbour.
1495.6	333.29	**for** fair genteman. Li **read** fair gentleman. Li
1516.3–4	334.13	**for** Walkup on **read** Walkup of Walkup on
1531.2–3	334.30–31	**for** executing an old **read** executing a charming old
1552.4	335.14	**for** that whiteyed kaffir? **read** that whiteeyed kaffir?
1561.11	335.24–5	**for** round to the **read** round the
1574.7	335.39	**for** the idea for **read** the ideas for
1587.1	336.14	**for** you about **read** you all about
1601.9	336.32	**for** for faith we **read** for ifaith we
1633.1–6	337.31	**transfer** – Who is Junius? says J.J. **to 337.28–9 as a separate paragraph following** offence, Crofton.
1670.1	338.31	**for** – You Jack? **read** – You, Jack?

1721.8	340.9	**for** introt in *Epiphania* **read** introit *in Epiphania*
1741.1	340.32	**for** – *Que fecit* **read** – *Qui fecit*
1744.7–8	340.35	**for** upon the blessed **read** upon that he blessed
1754.5	341.5	**for** looking round to **read** looking around to
1770.2	341.25	**for** sea up **read** sea and up
1771.1	341.27	**insert dialogue dash**
1828.10	343.12	**for** by *Rakoczy's March* **read** by *Rakóczsy's March*
1840.13–1841.4	343.26–7	**for** Pigeonhouse. *Visszontlátásra,* **read** Pigeonhouse, and the Poolbeg Light. *Visszontlátásra,*
1841.7	343.27	**for** *kedvés baratón! Visszontlátásra!* **read** *kedvés baratóm! Visszontlátásra!*
1848.4–5	343.34	**for** and J.G. paralysed **read** and J.J. paralysed
1852.6	343.38	**for** Joe. Stop. **read** Joe. Stop!
1873.9	344.21	**for** initials, coat **read** initials, crest, coat
1888.10	344.40	**for** *débris* human **read** *débris*, human
1890.5–7	344.42	**for** T.C. **read** T. and C.
1907.1	345.18	**for** old sheepface on **read** old sheepsface on
1915.3	345.28	**for** And he answered **read** And He answered

13: Nausicaa

32.9	346.39	**for** loaf of brown **read** loaf or brown

95.5	348.28	**for** not let **read** not to let
106.9	348.42	**for** eyes a **read** eyes, a
132.8	349.30	**for** him in the **read** him in in the
188.2–3	351.12	**for** yet and **read** yet – and
263.3	353.20	**for** the beetoteetom, laughed **read** the beeoteetom, laughed
301.1	354.24	**for** was the **read** was that the
323.5	355.8	**for** artistic standard, **read** artistic, standard,
340.7–8	355.28–9	**for** when there **read** when she went there
508.10	360.19	**for** and bit **read** and a bit
511.2–3	360.22	**for** shoulders, a **read** shoulders – a
513.15	360.25	**for** answering flush of **read** answering flash of
530.2	361.2	**for** their baby home **read** their babby home
579.6–7	362.17	**for** hurt. O **read** hurt – O
603.7–10	363.5–6	**for** them and **read** them and never would be and
611.12–15	363.15	**for** compliments on **read** compliments to all and sundry on
621.14	363.28	**for** put round him round **read** put round
639.1	364.6	**for** girlish treasures trove, **read** girlish treasure trove,
670.12	365.2	**for** follow her **read** follow, her
728.11	366.31	**for** back he **read** back that he
729.6	366.32	**for** knee no-one **read** knee where no-one
737.6	366.42	**for** blind and **read** blind blank and
740.10	367.3–4	**for** so lively! O **read** so lovely!

770.6–8	367.40	**for** because Gerty **read** because – because Gerty
776.8–9	368.5	**for** same. Wouldn't **read** same. I wouldn't
796.14	368.29–30	**for** her *deshabillé*. Excites **read** her *deshabille*. Excites
810.6	369.4	**for** other's neck or **read** other's necks or
812.4	369.6	**for** cool coif and **read** cool coifs and
842.13–843.2	369.41	**for** pound. All **read** pound. What? I think so. All
860.13–14	370.20	**for** behind coming **read** behind the wall coming
864.10–865.2	370.25	**for** you're in **read** you're stuck. Gain time. But then you're in
891.4	371.14–15	**for** After Gencree dinner **read** After Glencree dinner
922.12	372.10	**for** she carried parcels **read** she carries parcels
927.7	372.16	**for** nice face. Mullingar. **read** nice pace. Mullingar.
947.5	372.38	**for** *was Jemina Brown* **read** *was Jemima brown*
962.6	373.15	**for** And, Mrs **read** And Mrs
990.10	374.6	**for** it's arranged. **read** it's all arranged.
1009.2	374.27	**for** No, Hyacinth? **read** No. Hyacinth?
1019.11	374.40	**for** fine veil **read** fine fine veil
1020.12	374.41	**for** they're aways spinning **read** they're always spinning
1027.9	375.7	**for** oil or ether **read** oil of ether

1050.11	375.36	**for** do. Fellow run **read** do. Fellows run
1069.9	376.15–16	**for** Grace Darling. People **read** Grace darling. People
1146.11	378.23	**for** Nerve? they **read** Nerve they
1147.5	378.24	**for** back. Lot must **read** back. Lots must
1169.5	379.9–10	**for** of holding: hour **read** of folding: hour
1175.4	379.16–17	**for** *Cup race!* and **read** *Cup races!* and
1282.8–1283.6	382.17	**for** plump years **read** plump bubs me breadvan Winkle red slippers she rusty sleep wander years

14: Oxen of the Sun

5.7–8, 6.1	383.8	**for** Hoopsa, boyaboy, hoopsa. **read** Hoopsa boyaboy hoopsa!
8.9	383.10–11	**for** most profitable by **read** most profitably by
39.6	384.5	**for** been trembling **read** been the trembling
76.7	385.9–10	**for** Watchers they there **read** Watchers twey there
88.4	385.24	**for** nine year had **read** nine years had
134.15	386.37	**for** and reproved the **read** and repreved the
140.6	387.2	**for** and sometimes venery. **read** and sometime venery.
143.4	387.5	**for** move for **read** move more for
154.11	387.19	**for** was marvel **read** was a marvel
165.2	387.32	**for** neighbour wist not **read** neighbour nist not

306.3	391.38	**for** marriages *parce que M.* **read** marriages *parceque M.*
308.1	391.40	**for** *Entweder* transsubstantiality *oder* **read** *Entweder* transubstantiality *oder*
321.2	392.11–12	**for** that not gasteful **read** that no gasteful
357.3	393.13	**for** my truth, of **read** my troth, of
362.13	393.20	**for** effect, said Zarathustra, **read** effect, saith Zarathustra,
388.5	394.8–9	**for** things accord in **read** thing accords in
424.11	395.11	**for** the braggart's side **read** the braggart' side
434.9	395.22	**for** Indeed not for **read** Indeed no for
441.8–13	395.31	**for** he and make **read** he though he must nor would he make
480.14	396.36	**for** dry flags and **read** dry flag and
509.10	397.28–9	**for** in pair **read** in a pair
515.8	397.36	**for** issue. 'This her **read** issue. 'Tis her
532.6	398.14	**for** over to search **read** over the search
562.7	399.8	**for** favour or moonlight **read** favour of moonlight
562.11	399.8	**for** fecking maid's linen **read** fecking maids' linen
573.10	399.21	**for** hoose of the **read** hoose or the
586.8–9	399.37	**for** of gold **read** of cloth of gold
598.2	400.9	**for** tongue then lie **read** tongue than lie
609.2	400.22	**for** in bull's language **read** in bulls' language
634.1	401.11	**for** the bull's language **read** the bulls' language

679.10	402.25	**for** this inconvenience (which **read** this inconvenient (which
683.10	402.29–30	**for** of not much **read** of note much
698.12	403.5	**for** it. The both, **read** it. They both,
708.1	403.16–17	**for** *ut matres familiarum nostrae* **read** *ut matresfamiliarum nostrae*
727.1	403.39	**for** ask Mr **read** ask of Mr
742.14	404.16–17	**for** questioning pose of **read** questioning poise of
744.12	404.19	**for** the head, asked **read** the bottle asked
766.7	405.4	**for** of blessing to **read** of blessings to
791.8	405.33	**for** our heart and **read** our hearts and
873.1	408.6	**for** Writer express it) **read** Writer expresses it)
887.3	408.23	**for** Mr Crothers, clapping **read** Mr Crotthers, clapping
906.13	409.6	**for** to civil rights, **read** to civic rights,
931.1	409.35–6	**for** an opprobium in **read** an opprobrium in
954.11	410.22	**for** only bond of **read** only band of
963.7	410.32	**for** the agnatia of **read** the agnathia of
999.6	411.34	**for** knew know to **read** knew how to
1029.7	412.29	**for** of Mananaan! The **read** of Mananaun! The
1047.1	413.8	**for** in Clambrassil street **read** in Clanbrassil street
1061.6	413.25	**for** shrivels, to **read** shrivels, dwindles to

1075.10–11	413.42	**for** thee and **read** thee – and
1080.1	414.5	**for** of cycles of generations **read** of generations
1148.9	416.4	**for** that Periplepomenos sells **read** that Periplepomenes sells
1153.1	416.9	**for** that it is, **read** that she is,
204.5	417.29	**for** made. Crothers was **read** made. Crotthers was
1245.9	418.36	**for** These facts, he **read** These factors, he
1257.9	419.8	**for** to abnormal trauma **read** to abdominal trauma
1302.15	420.21	**for** in Mdw., F. **read** in Midw., F.
1354.1	421.41	**for** cut off **read** cut him off
1375.9	422.24	**for** of danger *read* of the danger
1404.7	423.17	**for** pallor. Them all **read** pallor. Then all
1430.3–4	424.6	**for** never do. **read** never – do.
1450.1	424.30	**for** gun. Burke's! Thence **read** gun. Burke's! Burke's! Thence
1450.9–1451.1	424.31	**for** foot where's **read** foot. Where's
1454.2	424.35	**for** Beatitudes! *Ratamplan Digidi* **read** Beatitudes! *Retamplan Digidi*
1458.9–10	424.41	**for** tramp the **read** tramp, tramp the
1459.3	424.41	**for** are (attitudes!) parching. **read** are (atitudes!) parching.
1462.9	425.3	**for** fall. Bishops' boosebox. **read** fall. Bishops boosebox.
1473.6	425.15–16	**for** he was settin **read** he wus settin

1500.7	426.5–6	**for** acoming, Underconstumble? **read** acoming. Underconstumble?
1504.8	426.10	**for** chile vely solly. **read** chile velly solly.
1505.13	426.12	**for** nae tha fou. **read** nae the fou.
1508.5	426.14	**for** teetee. Mowsing nowt **read** teetee. Bowsing nowt
1510.14	426.17	**for** of Castille. Rows **read** of Castile. Rows
1514.15	426.22	**for** Stephen. Hand **read** Stephen Hand
1532.7	427.1	**for** mon, wee **read** mon, a wee
1534.4–5	427.3–4	**for** *capiat posteriora nostra.* Closingtime, **read** *capiat posterioria nostria.* Closingtime,
1539.5,7	427.9	**for** Kristyann will yu help, yung **read** Kristyann wil yu help yung
1540.9	427.10	**for** crown off his **read** crown of his
1542.1–2	427.12	**for** puttiest longbreakyet. Item **read** puttiest longbreak yet. Item
1554.1	427.26	**for** Pardon? See him **read** Pardon? Seen him
1555.3	427.27–8	**for** Pore picanninies! Thou'll **read** Pore piccaninnies! Thou'll
1580.3–4	428.14	**for** coming washed **read** coming. Washed
1584.7–9	428.19	**for** Dowie, that's **read** Dowie, that's my name, that's

15: Circe

1.1, 9.9	429.1,10	**enclose the first narrative direction in parentheses**
2.3	429.2	**for** *uncobbled transiding set* **read** *uncobbled tramsiding set*

3.7	429.3–4	**for** *of flimsy houses* **read** *of grimy houses*
6.10	429.7	**for** *of coal and* **read** *of coral and*
20.10	429.21	**for** *gurgles.*) Grhahute! **read** *gurgles.*) Ghahute!
24.2	429.25	**for** (*Gobbing.*) Ghaghahest. **read** (*Gobbling.*) Ghaghahest.
26.3	429.27	**for** *between the railings,* **read** *between two railings,*
27.9	429.28–9	**for** *hat moves, groans,* **read** *hat snores, groans,*
30.8	430.2	**for** *rams the last* **read** *rams her last*
62.2	430.35	**for** *blond copper polls.* **read** *blond cropped polls.*
91.5	432.2	**for** And say the **read** And says the
98.5	432.10	**for** *Salvi facti i sunt.* **read** *Salvi facti sunt.*
105.11	432.18	**for** not odours, would **read** not odour, would
117.9	433.3	**for** bread and wine **read** bread or wine
151.1	434.7	**for** *bright arclamps. He* **read** *bright arclamp. He*
155.5	434.11	**for** *into Olhousen's, the* **read** *into Olhausen's, the*
161.3	434.17–18	**for** *his rib and* **read** *his ribs and*
178.1–2	435.3	**new indented narrative direction at** (*Two cyclists*
195.7–8	435.20	**for** the hattrick? **read** the hat trick?

196.1, 198.1	435.21–3	**indent** (*Bloom trickleaps* [...] *parcelled hand.*) **as a separate narrative direction and follow it with the speech heading** BLOOM **from 435.21**
202.7	435.27	**for** in tracks or **read** in track or
216.1	436.15	**for** *Buenos noches,* **read** *Bueñas noches,*
226.1–228.2 229.1–2	436.24	**following** I beg. **insert indented narrative direction** (*He leaps right, sackragman right.*) **plus speech heading** BLOOM **plus speech** I beg. **followed by** (*He swerves* [...] *and on.*) **repositioned as an indented narrative direction**
229.5	436.24	**for** *sidles, stepsaside, slips* **read** *sidles, stepaside, slips*
231.11	436.26	**for** a fingerpost planted **read** a signpost planted
240.1	437.4	**for** O! **read** O.
242.8–243.1	437.6–7	**for** *hands watch, fobpocket, bookpocket, pursepocket, sweets* **read** *hands watchfob, pocketbookpocket, pursepoke, sweets*
243.6	437.7	**for** *sin, potato soap.)* **read** *sin, potatosoap.)*
247.5	437.11	**for** *approaches sniffling, nose* **read** *approaches, sniffing, nose*
275.1	438.12	**for** you kaput, Leopoldleben. **read** you kaputt, Leopoldleben.
283.3	438.22	**for** (*In pantomine dame's* **read** (*In pantomime dame's*
283.7–8	438.23	**transfer** *widow Twankey's* **to 438.22 between** *mobcap,* **and** *crinoline*
285.4–5	438.24	**for** *her hair plaited in* **read** *her plaited hair in*

289.7	438.29–30	**for** *a shrievelled potato* **read** *a shrivelled potato*
311.10	439.23–4	**for** *her, excuses, desire,* **read** *her, excuse, desire,*
319.2	440.2	**for** Nebrakada! Feminimum. **read** Nebrakada! Femininum!
353.1–7	441.9–10	**transfer** *plump as a pampered pouter pigeon* **to the end of the narrative direction and read** Giovanni, *plump* [...] *pigeon.*)
386.3	442.21	**for** (*She slides away* **read** (*She glides away*
398.13	443.5–6	**for** think me? **read** think of me?
399.6	443.6	**for** have hears. How **read** Have ears. How
406.1	443.14	**for** very minute or **read** very sminute or
419.1–3	443.28–9	**insert speech heading** TOM AND SAM
433.3–4	444.11	**for** old sake'sake. I **read** Old sake' sake. I
466.1	445.20	**for** *and thumbs passing* **read** *and thumb passing*
479.1–2	446.6–10	**inset** (*Dennis Breen* [...] *in laughter.*) **as a narrative direction**
480.1	446.6–7	**for** *Hely's sandwichboard, shuffles* **read** *Hely's sandwichboards, shuffles*
496.8	446.25–6	**for** Mrs Bandman Palmer. **read** Mrs Bandmann Palmer.
498.5	446.28	**for** for pig's feet. **read** for pigs' feet.
559.2	449.9	**for** cruel creature, **read** cruel naughty creature,
600.1–603.9	450.24–7	**delete inset and read as four separate speeches**

662.7	453.4	**for** mad. Fido. Uncertain **read** mad. Dogdays. Uncertain
662.12–663.1–2	453.4–5	**for** movements. Good **read** movements. Good fellow! Fido! Good
672.6	453.15	**for** *lets unrolled* **read** *lets the unrolled*
678.3	453.21	**for** *lays a hand* **read** *lays hand*
711.2	454.24	**for** strangling pully will **read** strangling pulley will
721.13	455.6	**for** von Bloom Pasha. **read** von Blum Pasha.
740.11	455.27	**for** of Castille. Bloom. **read** of Castile. Bloom.
741.1	455.27	**for** name Virag. **read** name. Virag.
747.7	456.5	**for** in shake **read** in the shake
753.10	456.13	**for** Henry! Leopold! Leopold! Lionel, **read** Henry! Leopold! Lionel,
770.3	457.3	**for** *the past of* **read** *the pass of*
775.1	457.8	**for** Gentleman of **read** Gentlemen of
779.2	457.12–13	**for** gentleman, who do **read** gentleman, what do
812.5	458.19	**for** *Weekly Arsewiper* here. **read** *Weekly Arsewipe* here.
823.3	458.31	**for** a literateur. It's **read** a *littérateur*. It's
824.8	458.33	**for** bestselling books, really **read** bestselling copy, really
876.3	460.27	**for** *rumpled softly*.) **read** *rumpled: softly*.)
881.2	461.5	**for** them oysters! **read** them oylsters!
895.1	461.21	**for** GEORGES FOTTRELL **read** GEORGE FOTTRELL

899.4	461.25	**for** *long unintelligibe speech.* **read** *long unintelligible speech.*
916.7–8	462.16	**for** *pensums, model* **read** *pensums or model*
952.4–5	463.20	**for** unfold one **read** unfold – one
986.3	464.25	**for** *(The mirage of* **read** *(The image of*
1005.1–2	465.9	**position** *(A paper* [...] *into court.)* **as a separate narrative direction**
1031.10	466.5	**for** and ballstop **read** and the ballstop
1047.1	466.22	**for** coachman Balmer while **read** coachman Palmer while
1054.4–5,16	466.30–31	**enclose** stating that [...] urge me **in parentheses, not commas**
1081.10	467.28–9	**for** *of sudden fury.)* **read** *of fury.)*
1107.6	468.24	**for** *hands with* **read** *hands: with*
1122.4	469.12	**for** *Stephens, ringleted, passes* **read** *Stephens, ringletted, passes*
1173.1–2,9	471.8–9	**transfer** *(A black* [...] *his head.)* **to the beginning of the following narrative direction, and delete the redundant parentheses**
1177.1	471.15	**for** *H. Rumbold,* **read** *(H. Rumbold,*
1189.4	471.29–30	**for** Lewd chimpanzees. *(Breathlessly.)* **read** Lewd chimpanzee. *(Breathlessly.)*
1241.11	473.27–8	**for** Jacobs Vobiscuits. **read** Jacobs. Vobiscuits.
1246.12–13	474.5–6	**for** *forward, places* **read** *forward and places*
1247.9	474.6	**for** My masters' voice! **read** My master's voice!

1267.5–1268.9	474.27	**for** *again. He* **read** *again through the sump. Kisses chirp amid the rifts of fog. A piano sounds. He*
1273.3	475.3	**for** coocoo! Yummyumm Womwom! **read** coocoo! Yummyyum, Womwom!
1296.11	475.28–9	**for** *hand slides over* **read** *hand glides over*
1332.1–2– 1333.8	477.12–14	**treat** (*Murmuring singsong* [...] *and rosewater.*) **as a speech direction, and run on** *Schorach ani* [...] *benoith Hierushaloim.*
1399.9	479.30–31	**for** Cead mille Failte **read** Cead Mile Failte
1415.3–4	480.13–14	**for** *Dublin, the* **read** *Dublin, his lordship the*
1652.2,4–5	488.13	**for** *Tinct. mix. vom.,* 4 minims. **read** *Tinct. nux. vom.,* 5 minims.
1653.3	488.14	**for** *taraxel. lig.,* 30 **read** *taraxel. liq.,* 30
1658.8	488.19	**for** K.II. **read** K.11.
1691.6–8	490.1	**for** the universal **read** the universal language with universal
1693.3–4	490.2–3	**for** money, free **read** money, free rent, free
1732.1–3	491.14	**position** (*Laughter.*) **as a separate narrative direction**
1771.5–7	492.33	**for** *sgenl inn ban* **read** *sgeul im barr*
1805.12– 1806.2	494.6	**for** hairshirt winter **read** hairshirt of pure Irish manufacture winter
1813.2	494.15	**for** *coins, bank cheques,* **read** *coins, blank cheques,*
1823.4–5	494.26	**for** *All are* **read** *All the octuplets are*
1838.4–7	495.6	**for** a miracle. **read** a miracle like Father Charles.

1861.4	495.31–2	**for** Adrianopoli began Aranjuez **read** Adrianopoli begat Aranjuez
1872.1	496.11	**for** A CRAB **read** CRAB
1880.7	496.19	**for** *from front to* **read** *from frons to*
1893.4	497.5	**for** see kay **read** see Kay
1907.9	497.20	**for** Messiah! Abulafia! **read** Messiah! Abulafia! Recant!
1936.11–12	498.18–21	**reposition** (*He exhibits* [...] *of burning.*) **as a speech direction running on from** of Erin. **and position** (*The daughters* [...] *and pray.*) **as a separate narrative direction**
1953.10	499.4	**for** *by Mr Vincent* **read** *by Vincent*
1954.3–1955.2	499.5	**for** *the Alleluia chorus, accompanied* **read** *the chorus from Handel's Messiah* Alleluia for the Lord God omnipotent reigneth, *accompanied*
1974.15– 1975.4	499.28	**for** and bottle. **read** and bottle. I'm sick of it. Let everything rip.
1983.9	500.5	**for** pigs play the **read** pigs plays the
2007.3	501.4	**for** *tongue tolling and* **read** *tongue lolling and*
2035.3	502.7	**for** *is thrown open.* **read** *is flung open.*
2058.14	502.34	**for** *with the wand.* **read** *with his wand.*
2089.4	504.1	**for** illustrate *Caela enarrant* **read** illustrate *Coela enarrant*
2093.2–4	504.6	**for** about his **read** about the alrightiness of his
2117.16	505.3	**for** itself. God **read** itself, God
2163.7	506.27–8	**for** *Rien n'va plus.* **read** *Rien va plus.*
2166.5	506.31	**for** *torpor, crosses herself* **read** *torpor, crossing herself*

2167.1–2	507.1–3	**inset as a narrative direction**
2183.4	507.18	**for** *the passing drift* **read** *the possing drift*
2189.13	507.25	**for** Sue, Dave Campbell, **read** Sue, Dove Campbell,
2227.8–2228.1	508.33	**for** bishop. My **read** bishop and enrolled in the brown scapular. My
2234.1	509.5	**for** three stars I **read** three star. I
2247.8	509.21	**for** *in hairdresser attire,* **read** *in hairdresser's attire,*
2254.11	509.29	**for** know. Yeats **read** know, Yeats
2262.6	510.7	**for** *of Mananaan MacLir* **read** *of Mananaun MacLir*
2263.12	510.9	**for** *druid mantle. About* **read** *druid mouth. About*
2267.1	510.13	**for** MANANAAN MACLIR **read** MANANAUN MACLIR
2280.2	510.27	**for** Pooah! Pfuiiiiii! **read** Pooah! Pfuiiiiiii!
2373.3	514.4–5	**for** and Ichthyosaurus. For **read** and Ichthyosauros. For
2400.12	515.1	**for** of 1882 to **read** of 1886 to
2410.1	515.12	**for** then tomorrow as **read** then morrow as
2412.2	515.15	**for** *(Prompts into his ear in* **read** *(Prompts in*
2414.1	515.17	**for** pulchritudinous female possessing **read** pulchritudinous fumale possessing
2414.5	515.18	**for** pudendal verve in **read** pudendal nerve in
2427.3–9	515.33	**for** Charley! Buzz! **read** Charley! (*He blows in Bloom's ear.*) Buzz!
2441.8	516.13	**for** *wags head* **read** *wags his head*

2442.6–10	516.14	**for** my ocular. **read** my ocular. (*He sneezes.*) Amen!
2446.2	516.18	**for** serpent contradict. Not **read** serpent contradicts. Not
2453.6	516.26	**for** been the known ... **read** been the the known ...
2462.1–2	516.35	**for** Who's Ger Ger? Who's **read** Who's moth moth? Who's
2462.6–14	516.35	**for** Gerald? O, **read** Gerald? Dear Ger, that you? O dear, he is Gerald. O,
2465.6	517.3	**for** *mews.*) Luss puss **read** *mews.*) Puss puss
2467.2–11	517.5	**for** rest anon. **read** rest anon. (*He snaps his jaws suddenly in the air.*)
2468.1–2	517.5–6	**insert speech heading** THE MOTH
2477.1–7	517.13–14	**position** Pretty pretty [...] pretty petticoats. **as a separate line, inset**
2478.8	517.15	**for** *two sliding steps* **read** *two gliding steps*
2538.9	519.15	**for** the by have **read** the bye have
2554.3	520.2	**for** man grasps woman's **read** man grapses woman's
2573.7	520.22–3	**for** Judas Iacchias, a **read** Judas Iacchia, a
2614.7–8	522.8	**for** Ben MacChree! **read** Ben my Chree!
2649.7	523.20	**for** sure you are a **read** sure you're a
2672.1	524.19	**for** Hi-hi-hi-hi-his legs **read** Hihihihihis legs
2677.7	524.24	**for** *swarms over* **read** *swarms white over*
2702.7	525.18	**for** *briskly.*) Hum. Thank **read** *briskly.*) Hmmm! Thank

2714.1–2	526.1–2	**position** (*She tosses* [...] *a crack.*) **as a separate narrative direction**
2734.5	526.22	**for** *heelclacking is* **read** *heelclacking tread is*
2736.7–9	526.24	**for** Aphrodisiac? But **read** Aphrodisiac? Tansy and pennyroyal. But
2736.12	526.24	**for** I thought it. **read** I bought it.
2751.4	527.11	**for** *glances around her* **read** *glances round her*
2764.7	527.25	**for** *her eardrop.*) **read** *her left eardrop.*)
2766.1–2	527.28	**for** Yes. No. **read** Nes. Yo.
2769.15	528.4	**for** now we? **read** now me?
2806.12	529.16	**for** for Kellet's. Experienced **read** for Kellett's. Experienced
2814.10	529.23	**for** in Mansfield's was **read** in Manfield's was
2816.9	529.26	**for** incredibly small, **read** incredibly impossibly small,
2827.2	530.7	**for** luck. Nook in **read** luck. Hook in
2845.6	531.2	**for** *semiflexed.*) Magnificence. **read** *semiflexed.*) Magmagnificence!
2851.10–11	531.8–9	**for** *closing.*) Truffles! **read** *closing, yaps.*) Truffles!
2860.13	531.19	**for** *in.*) Feel **read** *in.*) Footstool! Feel
2882.6	532.11	**for** dear. I **read** dear, I
2898.5	532.29–30	**for** *Victualler's* Gazette. Very **read** *Victualler's Gazette.* Very
2901.10–11	533.2–3	**run on** (*He twists* [...] *turning turtle.*) **as a speech direction following** hurt you.

2902.1	533.3	**for** *Bloom squeaks, turning* **read** *Bloom squeals, turning*
2929.1–2	534.4–5	**reposition** (*They hold and pinion Bloom.*) **as a separate narrative direction**
2932.12	534.7–8	**for** elected chairman of **read** elected vicechairman of
2934.8	534.10	**for** that I didn't **read** that didn't
2947.3–4	534.24	**for** *in the saddle.* **read** *in the, in the saddle.*
2959.1	535.6	**for** *farts loudly.*) Take **read** *farts stoutly.*) Take
2985.2	536.5	**for** (*A charming soubrette* **read** (*Charming soubrette*
2986.13	536.7	**for** only once, a **read** only twice, a
2997.1	536.19	**for** Miriam, Black **read** Miriam. Black
3003.8	536.26	**for** liftboy, Henry Fleury **read** liftboy, Henri Fleury
3032.6	537.24	**for** he encouraged **read** he frankly encouraged
3045.1	538.6	**for** *Booloohoom. Poldy* **read** *Booloohoom, Poldy*
3047.1–4	538.8	**for** *other, the ...)* **read** *other the, lane the.*)
3055.8	538.17	**for** Two! Thr ... ! **read** Two! Thr ...
3068.15–3069.1	539.2–3	**for** Say, thank you mistress. **read** Say, *thank you mistress.*
3095.1–3096.1	540.1–2	**transfer** THE LACQUEY Barang! **to 539.32–3 following** *his handbell.*)
3103.8,11	540.7–8	**for** examine his points. Handle him. This **read** examine shis points. Handle hrim. This
3119.11	540.26	**for** Louis XV heels, **read** Louis Quinze heels,

3121.5	540.28	**for** your power of **read** your powers of
3158.2–3,5	542.7	**for** Rip Van Winkle! Rip Van Winkle! **read** Rip van Wink! Rip van Winkle!
3171.4	542.21	**for** But. O **read** But, O
3176.5–6	542.26–7	**for** you, say? Following **read** you, eh, following
3186.4	543.7–8	**for** for art's sake. **read** for art' sake.
3202.8–9	543.25–6	**reposition** (*He bites his thumb.*) **as a speech direction running on from** Has nobody … ?
3215.15–16	544.12–13	**reposition** (*He weeps tearlessly.*) **as a speech direction running on from** have suff …
3223.8	544.21	**for** *Watchman, O.Mastiansky,* **read** *Watchman, P.Mastiansky,*
3224.5	544.21–2	**for** *Abramovitz, Chazen. With* **read** *Abramovitz, chazen. With*
3227.2	544.25	**for** (*In a dark* **read** (*In dark*
3273.10	546.17	**for** of my bed **read** of bed
3285.7	547.2	**for** *her hand.*) What **read** *her hands.*) What
3310.1–3314.1	548.4–5	**following** our shade? **insert** BLOOM (*Scared.*) High School of Poula? Mnemo? Not in full possession of faculties. Concussion. Run over by tram. THE ECHO Sham!
3321.4–5, 3322.4–5	548.12,13	**enclose** for they love […] unbridles vice **in parentheses, and read** stairs (for […] vice), even
3321.9	548.12	**for** crushes, instincts of **read** crushes, instinct of

3331.6–7	548.23–4	**reposition** (*They cheer.*) **as a speech direction running on from** Hurray!
3333.5	548.26	**for** *mammamufflered, stunned with* **read** *mammamufflered, starred with*
3353.6	549.16	**for** The fauns. I **read** The fauna. I
3358.13	549.23	**for** and I ... A **read** and I. A
3363.1–10	549.28	**add initial speech direction** (*Large teardrops rolling from his prominent eyes, snivels.*)
3365.5	550.2	**for** need. (*With* **read** need I ... (*With*
3370.4	550.7	**for** (*Bleats.*) Megegaggegg! Nannannanny! **read** (*Bleats.*) Megeggaggegg! Nannannanny!
3372.10	550.9–10	**for** *and gorsepine.*) Regularly **read** *and gorsespine.*) Regularly
3377.1–2	550.13–16	**reposition** (*Through silversilent* [...] *waiting waters.*) **as a separate narrative direction**
3378.3	550.14–15	**for** *rolls rotatingly from* **read** *rolls roteatingly from*
3381.1	550.18	**for** Bbbbbllllbbblblodschbg? **read** Bbbbbllllblblblblobschb!
3390.2	550.28	**for** Done. Prff. **read** Done. Prff!
3397.2	551.8	**for** (*Pacing the* **read** (*Pawing the*
3418.2	552.2	**for** (*From the* **read** (*In the*
3439.7	552.24	**for** *back trousers' button snaps.*) **read** *back trouserbutton snaps.*)
3456.1–12	553.14	**precede** Sacrilege! To **with a new speech direction** (*Her features hardening, gropes in the folds of her habit.*)
3459.2	553.16	**for** *clutches in* **read** *clutches again in*

3463.11	553.21	**for** Cat of nine **read** Cat o' nine
3464.13	553.23	**for** do we lack **read** do you lack
3475.13	554.3	**for** Eh! I **read** Eh? I
3477.14	554.6	**for** *sniffs.*) But. Onions. *Read sniffs.*) Rut. Onions.
3484.4	554.12	**for** superfluous hairs. A **read** superfluous hair. A
3490.1	554.19	**for** *barks.*) Fohracht! **read** *barks.*) Fbracht!
3492.10– 3493.1	554.21–2	**for** first, the cold spunk of your bully is **read** first, your bully's cold spunk is
3513.9	555.17	**for** still a **read** still, a
3542.6–8	556.22	**for** *money, then* **read** *money, then at Stephen, then*
3549.5–6	556.29	**for** *Zoe bounds over to the* **read** *Zoe bends over the*
3575.1–2	557.27–8	**reposition** (*He lifts* [...] *the sofa.*) **as a separate narrative direction**
3588.4	558.15	**for** (*Points.*) Hum? Deep **read** (*Points.*) Him? Deep
3589.1–2	558.15–17	**reposition** (*Lynch bends* [...] *to Stephen.*) **as a separate narrative direction**
3628.5	560.2	**for** *match nearer his* **read** *match near his*
3642.3	560.19	**for** *it into the*) **read** *it in the*)
3653.4	560.30	**for** alle kaput. **read** alle kaputt.
3656.1–2	561.3	**for** Blue eyed beauty, I'll **read** Blue eyes beauty I'll
3710.5–6	563.9–10	**run on** (*She sidles* [...] *waddles off.*) **as a speech direction following** Klook. Klook.

3718.9–3719.2 563.17   **for** twentytwo too. **read** twentytwo. Sixteen years ago he was twentytwo too.

3737.6–8   564.10–11   **for** (*They whisper again.*) **read** (*She whispers again.*) **and run on as a speech direction following** *Florry.*) Whisper.

3739.9   564.13–14   **for** *in a yachtsman's* **read** *in yachtsman's*

3741.2   564.15   **for** *Boylan's shoulder.*) **read** *Boylan's coat shoulder.*)

3746.2   564.20   **for** (*Seated, smiles.*) **read** (*Sated, smiles.*)

3758.3   565.7   **for** Bloom up yet? **read** Bloom dressed yet?

3760.2,4   565.9   **for** (*In a flunkey's plum plush* **read** (*In flunkey's prune plush*

3782.1–3784.5 566.5–6   **insert** BOYLAN
(*Clasps himself.*) Here, I can't hold this little lot much longer. (*He strides off on stiff cavalry legs.*)

3792.8   566.14   **for** *holds an* **read** *holds out an*

3809.12–3810.1   567.4–5   **for** Ah! Gooblazqruk brukarchkrasht! **read** Ah! Godblazegrukbrukarchkhrasht!

3812.10–3813.1   567.7–8   **for** Weeshwashtkissima pooisthnapoohuck! **read** Weeshwashtkissinapooisthnapoohuck!

3829.1   567.25–6   **for** his Thursdaymomun. Iagogogo! **read** his Thursdaymornun. Iagogogo!

3831.6   568.2   **for** *the whores.*) **read** *the three whores.*)

3836.2   568.7   **for** taken near the **read** taken next the

3842.7,11   568.14   **for** *Scottish widow's insurance policy and large* **read** *Scottish Widows' insurance policy and a large*

3843.8   568.15   **for** *brood runs with* **read** *brood run with*

3844.11	568.16	**for** *one short foot,* **read** *one shod foot,*
3858.4	568.30	**for** *bowing, twisting japanesily.*) **read** *bowing, twirling japanesily.*)
3880.10	569.24	**for** Rmm Rrrrrrmmmmm. **read** Rmm Rrrrrrmmmm.
3883.1	569.27	**for** to expenses your **read** to expense your
3884.2	570.1	**for** perhaps her heart **read** perhaps hers heart
3894.1–2	570.13	**for** *Ho, la la! Ce* **read** *Ho, là là! Ce*
3900.1,9	570.19	**for** *(Grimacing with [...] clapping himself.)* **read** *(With head back, laughs loudly, clapping himself grimacing.)*
3906.4–5	570.26	**for** lifesize tompeeptoms virgins **read** lifesize tompeeptom of virgins
3907.8	570.27–8	**for** in mirrors every **read** in mirror every
3909.7	570.30	**for** or omelette on **read** or omlet on
3928.2	571.17	**for** Dreams go by **read** Dreams goes by
3930.2	571.19	**for** *(Extending his* **read** *(Extends his*
3941.3	572.8	**for** *sharpened.)* Hola! Hillyho! **read** *sharpened.) Holà!* Hillyho!
3950.9	572.18–19	**for** Bulbul! Burblblbrurblbl! Hai, **read** Bulbul! Burblblburblbl! Hai,
3951.11	572.20–21	**for** *rapidly across country. A* **read** *rapidly crosscountry. A*
3958.7	572.28	**for** *sticks, salmongaffs,* **read** *sticks, hayforks, salmongaffs,*
3968.5,10	573.5	**for** bar one. [...] bar one. **read** bar one! [...] bar one!
3979.4–5	573.17	**for** *their saddles.* **read** *their, in their saddles.*

3989.4   573.28–9   **for** *at a schooling* **read** *at schooling*

3989.8   573.29–30   **run on** *Per vias rectas!* **following** *schooling gallop.*)

4002.5   574.10   **for** sort a **read** sort of a

4008.1   574.16   **for** Who'll ... **read** Who'll ... ?

4024.3   575.8   **for** (*Twirls around herself,* **read** (*Twirls round herself,*

4025.3–5   575.9   **for** dance? **read** dance? Clear the table.

4027.1   575.11   **for** *prelude to* My **read** *prelude of* My

4028.5   575.12   **for** *Zoe around the* **read** *Zoe round the*

4030.6   575.14–15   **for** *her around the* **read** *her round the*

4030.9–11   575.16   **transfer** *Bloom stands aside.* **to 575.15 following** *the room.*

4037.11–   575.23   **for** *is a dahlia.* **read** *is an immense dahlia.*
4038.1

4039.12   575.25   **for** *hand limply on* **read** *hand lightly on*

4044.4   575.30   **for** Lanner steps. So. **read** Lanner step. So.

4045.13   575.32   **for** *monde an avant!* **read** *monde en avant!*

4048.2   575.35   **for** *shrivels, shrinks, his* **read** *shrivels, sinks, his*

4049.3   575.36   **for** *time, pounds. Stephen* **read** *time, sounds. Stephen*

4050.3–5   575.37   **for** *fade, gold, rose, violet.*) **read** *fade, gold rosy violet.*)

4055.1   576.4–5   **for** *goldhaired, slim, in* **read** *goldhaired, slimsandalled, in*

4060.11   576.12   **for** evenly! *Balance!* **read** evenly! *Balancé!*

4080.1	577.2	**for** *Avant! huit!* **read** *Avant huit!*
4081.4–7	577.3	**for** *hours steal* **read** *hours, one by one, steal*
4088.2	577.10	**for** *(Twisting, her* **read** *(Twirling, her*
4092.3	577.14	**for** *curtseying, twisting, simply* **read** *curtseying, twirling, simply*
4100.2	577.22	**for** *each with* **read** *each each with*
4109.14	578.2–3	**for** the Mirus bazaar! **read** the *Mirus* bazaar!
4117.1–5	578.11–12	**delete inset and run on** Come on all! **to follow** and through.
4126.5	578.22	**for** *flashes. Toft's* **read** *flashes Toft's*
4133.1	578.29	**for** *they scotlootshoot lumbering* **read** *they scootlootshoot lumbering*
4144.3–4	579.11	**for** coffin. Steel **read** coffin steel
4148.8	579.16	**for** *last wiswitchback lumbering* **read** *last switchback lumbering*
4153.8	579.21–2	**for** *on wall. He* **read** *on walls. He*
4176.8	580.15	**for** you? What **read** you? No. What
4178.12,14	580.18–19	**for** Kinch killed her dosgbody bitchbody. She **read** Kinch dogsbody killed her bitchbody. She
4180.1–2	580.20	**for** *eyes into the* **read** *eyes on to the*
4186.10	580.27	**for** They said I **read** They say I
4214.4–6	581.28	**for** *(Panting.)* The **read** *(Panting.)* His noncorrosive sublimate! The
4219.4–6	582.4–5	**for** *outstretched fingers.)* Beware! God's **read** *outstretched finger.)* Beware God's

4220.1–2	582.5–6	**reposition** (*A green* [...] *Stephen's heart.*) **as a separate narrative direction**
4223.1–12	582.8–9	**in place of these lines read** (*Strangled with rage, his features drawn grey and old.*) Shite!
4256.6	583.17	**for** *and flees from* **read** *and flies from*
4260.8	583.21	**for** *the halldoors. Lynch* **read** *the halldoor. Lynch*
4268.12–13	584.2–3	**for** *coattail.) There. You* **read** *coattail.) Here, you*
4279.5	584.13	**for** Didn't he ... ! **read** Didn't he ... ?
4284.3	584.18	**for** (*His hand under* **read** (*His head under*
4284.10	584.18	**for** *chain. Pulling, the* **read** *chain. Puling, the*
4290.16	584.25	**for** not a sixpenceworth **read** not sixpenceworth
4303.7–8	585.10–11	**for** here? Where **read** here or? Where
4306.12	585.14–15	**for** Oxford! (*Warningly.*) **read** Oxford? (*Warningly.*)
4308.6–7	585.17	**for** are you incog? **read** are. Incog!
4312.12	585.21–2	**for** *and shouts.) That's* **read** *and starts.) That's*
4322.4	586.2	**for** *a ghostly lewd* **read** *a ghastly lewd*
4330.7	586.11	**for** *trousers, follows from* **read** *trousers, follow from*
4336.6,8	586.18	**for** *leader: 65 C 66 C night* **read** *leader: 65 C, 66 C, night*

4340.1,3 4341.1	586.22–3	**for** *Garryowen, Whatdoyoucallhim, Strangeface, Fellowthatslike, Sawhimbefore, Chapwith, Chris* **read** *Garryowen, Whodoyoucallhim, Strangeface, Fellowthatsolike, Sawhimbefore, Chapwithawen, Chris*
4347.1–2	586.29–30	**for** *Holohan, man in the street, other man in the street, Footballboots,* **read** *Holohan, maninthestreet, othermaninthestreet, Footballboots,*
4356.8	586.40	**for** *Drimmie's, colonel* **read** *Drimmie's, Wetherup, colonel*
4364.4	587.6	**for** Hi! Stop him on **read** Hi! Stophim on
4371.1	587.13	**for** guests. The uninvited. By **read** guests. Uninvited. By
4378.4–9	587.22	**for** didn't. The girls telling lies. He **read** didn't. I seen him. The girl there. He
4379.2,4	587.23	**for** up? Soldiers and civilians. **read** up? Soldier and civilian.
4381.15	587.26	**for** know and **read** know, and
4382.4	587.26	**for** man ran up **read** man run up
4387.5–7	587.30	**for** *of Kitty's and Lynch's heads.)* **read** *of Lynch's and Kitty's heads.)*
4388.7	587.31	**for** Poetic. Neopoetic. **read** Poetic. Uropoetic.
4384.1–4385.1	588.1–2	**transfer** VOICES Shesfaithfultheman. **(spelled thus in one word) to 587.28–9 following** shilling whore.
4396.2–4	588.12	**for** *(In* **read** *(Gentleman poet in*
4397.3	588.12–13	**for** *flowingbearded.) Their's not* **read** *flowingbearded.) Theirs not*
4405.11	588.22	**for** the private. **read** the privates.

4410.5	588.27	**for** *awry, advancing to* **read** *awry, advances to*
4413.4	589.2	**for** *up in the* **read** *up to the*
4429.2–3	589.19–20	**run on** (*He staggers a pace back.*) **as a speech direction following** perpendicular.
4435.3–4	589.26	**for** but modern philirenists, **read** but but human philirenists,
4443.5	590.7	**for** with much marked **read** with such marked
4462.7	590.30	**for** a back. **read** a bak.
4462.8–9, 4463.6–4464.2	590.30–591.3	**run on** (*He shakes* [...] *and Lynch.*) **as a speech direction following** a back. **and position** (*General applause* [...] *in acknowledgement.*) **as a separate narrative direction, inserting the two additonal parentheses**
4464.8	591.3	**for** *lifts the bucket* **read** *lifts his bucket*
4471.1	591.9	**for** patent medicine. A **read** patent medicines. A
4472.3–4	591.10–11	**for** country, suppose. (*He* **read** country. Suppose. (*He*
4474.7	591.13	**for** I don't want **read** I didn't want
4486.13	591.27–8	**for** saying. Taking a **read** saying. Taken a
4487.7–8	591.28–9	**for** absinthe, the greeneyed **read** absinthe. Greeneyed
4526.4	593.13	**for** a cove **read** a dove
4528.4	593.15	**for** the throat **read** the throats
4535.2	593.22	**for** But love **read** But I love
4537.8	593.24–5	**for** *with a gladstone* **read** *with gladstone*

4541.10, 4542.1	593.29–30	**for** from the body of Miss Barrow which **read** from body of Miss Barron which
4547.1–6	594.5	**for** *Horhot ho hray ho rhother's hest.* **read** Horhot ho hray hor hother's hest.
4555.5–6	594.13	**for** time as **read** time. As
4555.9	594.13	**for** to His Royal **read** to Her Royal
4582.5	595.11	**for** you, grammer! Hamlet, **read** you, gammer! Hamlet,
4597.13	595.28	**for** any bugger says **read** any fucker says
4620.1–4624.2	596.4–8	**transfer** THE CITIZEN *Erin go bragh!* (*Major Tweedy* [...] *fierce hostility.*) **to** **596.28–597.1 following** hashbaz.
4613.8,4614.4	596.23	**for** *with epaulette, gilt chevrons and sabretache, his* **read** *with epaulettes, gilt chevrons and sabretaches, his*
4618.12	596.27–8	**for** them! Mahal shalal **read** them! Mahar shalal
4628.2	597.4	**for** (*Waves the* **read** (*Moves the*
4649.1	597.25	**for** sacred lifegiver. **read** sacred lifegiver!
4680.6	598.33–4	**for** *rains dragon's teeth.* **read** *rains dragons' teeth.*
4688.2	599.8	**for** *The Donoghue. On* **read** *The O'Donoghue. On*
4693.10	599.14	**for** *a long petticoat* **read** *a lace petticoat*
4705.7	599.28	**for** *celebrant's petticoats, revealing* **read** *celebrant's petticoat, revealing*
4722.1–13	600.14–15	**transfer** (*The retriever* [...] *barks noisily.*) **from 601.26–7 to follow** fucking windpipe!

4736.1–4739.4	600.15–18	**transfer** OLF GUMMY [...] take him! **to 601.5–6 following** pure reason.
4728.1–2	600.23–4	**reposition** (*He drags Kitty away.*) **as a separate narrative direction**
4747.6	601.14	**for** *Stephen, fists outstretched,* **read** *Stephen, fist outstretched,*
4770.6–7	602.13	**for** Here bugger off, Harry. There's the **read** Here. Bugger off, Harry. Here's the
4775.5–6,9–10	602.19	**for** lady and he insulted us and assaulted **read** lady. And he insulted us. And assaulted
4793.12	603.13–14	**for** Bennett'll have you **read** Bennett'll shove you
4799.2	603.19	**for** (*Taking out* **read** (*Takes out*
4814.6	604.9	**for** cup. Throwaway. (*He* **read** cup. *Throwaway.* (*He*
4847.10	605.16	**for** have had to **read** have to
4856.1–2	605.26–7	**reposition** (*They move* [...] *heavy tread.*) **as a separate narrative direction following** gentlemen.
4863.3–4	606.8	**for** grief and **read** grief. And
4883.8	606.31–607.1	**for** a specialty. Will **read** a speciality. Will
4888.5	607.6	**for** *Bloom in* **read** *Bloom, in*
4920.4–6	608.12–13	**for** *their tooralooloolooloo lay.* **read** *their tooralooloo looloo lay.*
4930.2,6–7	608.23	**for** (*Groans.*) Who? Black panther vampire. **read** (*Frowns.*) Who? Black panther. Vampire.
4938.5	608.33	**for** *light hands and* **read** *light hand and*
4943.4–5	609.4	**for** dim ... **read** dim sea.

4945.2	609.6	**for** *holding his hat* **read** *holding the hat*
4951.7	609.13	**for** him ... (*He* **read** him. (*He*
4953.3	609.15	**for** *murmers*.) in **read** *murmers*.) ... in

16: Eumaeus

6.13	613.7	**for** no pumps of **read** no pump of
19.1, 20.11	613.22–4	**transfer** brushing **from 613.24 to 613.22 and read** preliminaries as brushing, in spite [...] shaving line, they both
33.10	613.40	**for** by Mullet's and **read** by Mullett's and
43.9	614.9	**for** returning the **read** returning and the
59.3–4	614.28	**for** bread? At **read** bread at
67.10	614.38	**for** little juijitsu for **read** little jiujitsu for
70.7	614.41–2	**for** unconscious that, but **read** unconscious but
74.12	615.4	**for** or Malony which **read** or Mahony which
98.6–7	615.33	**for** Judas, said Stephen, who **read** Judas, Stephen said, who
101.12	615.37	**for** bridge when a **read** bridge where a
109.7	616.3	**for** a quondam friend **read** a *quondam* friend
114.1, 115.1	616.8	**transfer** *Night!* **to a separate line with a dialogue dash and in roman not italic, and begin a new paragraph with** Stephen, of
119.6	616.13	**for** least. Although unusual **read** least. Though unusual
121.6	616.16	**for** be about waylaying **read** be abroad waylaying

129.6	616.25	**for** in any over **read** in an over
136.1,3	616.33	**enclose** though not proved **in parentheses, not commas**
138.7	616.36	**for** seeing, his mother **read** seeing, her mother
138.13–139.8	616.37	**for** relative had **read** relative, a woman, as the tale went, of extreme beauty, had
147.9–11	617.3	**for** sprinkling of **read** sprinkling of a number of
157.6	617.14	**for** or the next **read** or next
158.9	617.15–16	**for** Mr Garret Deasy. **read** Mr Garrett Deasy.
161.12–14	617.19	**for** laugh. Got **read** laugh. I got
176.1	617.35–6	**for** *disco,* etcetera, as **read** *disco, etcetera,* as
181.7–8	617.42	**for** needful – whereas. He **read** needful. Whereas. He
190.2–3	618.10	**for** recollect about **read** recollect. About
191.1–3	618.11	**for** them, or **read** them he wondered, or
195.13	618.15	**for** Stephen lent **read** Stephen anyhow lent
197.11	618.18	**for** back some time. **read** back one time.
221.9	619.3–4	**for** impecuniosity. Probably he **read** impecuniosity. Palbably he
233.1–2	619.18	**for** – He's down **read** – He is down
245.1	619.33	**for** – Needs, Mr **read** – Needs! Mr
247.7	619.35–6	**for** needs and everyone **read** needs or everyone
262.1	620.9	**for** quite legitimately, out **read** quite legitimate, out

267.6–9	620.15–16	**for** confusion. **read** confusion, which they did.
309.7	621.23	**for** urinal he perceived **read** urinal they perceived
314.1	621.28	**for** – *Putana madonna,* **read** – *Puttana madonna,*
317.1	621.31–2	**insert speech** – *Mezzo.*
319.1–6	621.32–3	**insert speech** – *Ma ascolta! Cinque la testa più ...*
324.6–7	621.38	**for** he wouldn't vouch **read** he could not vouch
337.8	622.11	**for** individual, a portion **read** individual, portion
339.11	622.14	**no new paragraph at** Mr Bloom,
342.14–343.1	622.17	**for** voice, *apropos* of **read** voice, *à propos* of
347.1–2	622.22	**for** *Belladonna voglio.* **read** *Belladonna. Voglio.*
349.1	622.24	**for** from dead lassitude **read** from lassitude
363.3,6	622.41–2	**full stops, not commas, after** Podmore [...] Goodbody
393.1	623.31	**for** – Bottle out **read** – Bottles out
398.1, 401.1	623.37,40	**for** – Pom, he **read** – Pom! he **(twice)**
415.7–8	624.15	**for** continued, W.B. **read** continued, D.B.
419.4–11	624.19	**for** from. My **read** from. I belongs there. That's where I hails from. My
428.13	624.31	**for** way? Never **read** way. Never
437.1	624.40	**for** father. Boo! The **read** father. Broo! The
440.3	625.2	**for** husband, W.B. **read** husband, D.B.

443.13	625.6	**for** about you, do you? **read** about you?
452.5–6	625.15	**for** See? W.B. **read** See? D.B.
454.6	625.18	**for** his neighbours a **read** his neighbour a
460.5–11	624.24–5	**for** America. I **read** America. We was chased by pirates one voyage. I
463.6	625.27–8	**for** *Gospodi pomilooy.* That's **read** *Gospodi pomilyou.* That's
475.5,8	625.42	**for** attention on the scene exhibited, at a **read** attention at the scene exhibited, a
479.4	626.4	**for** day long, the **read** day, the
481.3	626.6	**for** them there **read** them sitting there
484.9	626.10	**for** inquired genially. **read** inquired generally.
491.1	626.17	**new paragraph at** Though not
515.6	627.3–4	**for** improvement tower **read** improvement, tower
525.9	627.16	**for** with its own **read** with his own
541.7	627.34–5	**for** for a matter **read** for the matter
543.2–3	627.36	**for** always cooped **read** always and ever cooped
568.11–12	628.24	**for** card picture and **read** card, picture, and
573.12	628.30	**for** the Chinese does. **read** the Chinks does.
582.4	628.40	**for** he. Chuck! It **read** he. Chuk! It
585.1	629.1	**new paragraph, with dialogue dash, at** That's a
594.3	629.12	**for** Mr Bloom and **read** Mr B. and
600.8–9	629.19	**for** Funny very. **read** Funny, very!

601.11	629.20–21	**for** reading by fits **read** reading in fits
606.1	629.25–6	**for** yesterday, some **read** yesterday, roughly some
618.8–9	629.41–2	**for** Mr Bloom interpolated. Can **read** Mr B. interrogated. Can
643.15	630.29	**for** a very laudable **read** a highly laudable
666.2	631.12	**for** The Skibbereen father **read** The Skibereen father
672.4	631.18	**for** buggers. Sucks your **read** buggers. Suck your
681.10–682.1	631.31	**for** the someway **read** the. Someway
694.5–6	632.1	**for** work, longshoreman one said. **read** work, one longshoreman said.
699.5	632.6	**for** number. A **read** number. Ate. A
716.7	632.27–8	**for** admit that he **read** admit he
740.2	633.15	**for** said that it **read** said it
745.10	633.22	**for** of that sort, **read** of the sort,
746.9	633.23	**for** lasting boom on **read** lasting boon on
768.7–11	634.9	**for** man I mean. The **read** man, I mean, the
785.11–12	634.30	**for** it and **read** it. And
809.4–11	635.16–17	**for** puddle – it clopped out of it when taken up – by **read** puddle it clopped out of when taken up by
815.8	635.24	**for** But oblige **read** But O, oblige
822.4	635.33	**for** his *confidente sotto* **read** his *confidante sotto*
854.4–5	636.29	**for** outline, the **read** outline of the

906.11	638.4	**for** wreck of Daunt's **read** wreck off Daunt's
911.8–9	638.10	**for** the Irish *Times*) **read** the *Irish Times*)
933.4	638.35	**for** exploit, gazing up **read** exploit, gaping up
938.12	638.42	**for** himself close at **read** himself closer at
940.6	639.2	**for** apparently woke a **read** apparently awoke a
940.12	639.2–3	**no new paragraph at** A hoof
943.1–2	639.5	**for** corporation, who **read** corporation stones, who
948.8	639.12	**for** hard times in **read** hard lines in
966.11–12	639.33	**for** Ask her captain, **read** Ask the then captain,
985.2	640.12–13	**no new paragraph at** Skin-the-Goat,
990.2	640.18–19	**for** million pounds' worth **read** million pounds worth
996.7	640.26	**for** in Cavan growing **read** in Navan growing
1049.2	642.3	**for** he (Bloom) couldn't **read** he (B.) couldn't
1060.1,12	642.17–18	**enclose** though, personally [...] such thing **in parentheses**
1063.9	642.21	**for** mortal (the man having **read** mortal (he having
1066.6	642.24–5	**for** nicknamed Skin-the-Goat, merely **read** nicknamed Skin-the, merely
1094.4	643.14	**for** Mr Bloom proceeded **read** Mr B. proceeded
1099.11	643.21	**for** violence or intolerance **read** violence and intolerance
1106.1	643.28	**delete dialogue dash**

1107.8	643.30	**for** was overwhelmingly full **read** was full
1116.2	643.40	**for** accuse – remarked **read** accuse, remarked
1117.1	643.40	**new paragraph at** He turned
1124.7–1125.1	644.6	**for** are practical **read** are imbued with the proper spirit. They are practical
1138.11	644.23	**for** a small smattering **read** a smattering
1139.3	644.23–4	**for** classical day in **read** classical days in
1148.8	644.34	**for** meaning to work. **read** meaning work.
1177.8	645.25–6	**for** Mr Bloom attached **read** Mr B attached
1216.10	646.31	**for** was interest **read** was his interest
1235.10	647.12	**for** addressed to A. **read** addressed A.
1242.4–10	647.20	**for** Ascot *Throwaway* **read** Ascot meeting, the Gold Cup. Victory of outsider *Throwaway*
1243.6	647.20–21	**for** when Captain Marshall's **read** when Capt. Marshall's
1252.4	647.31	**for** *as great* **read** *as a great*
1254.4,13	647.33–4	**transfer** *by* **to precede the parenthesis, and read** *out by* (certainly [...] Corny) *Messrs.*
1256.8	647.36	**for** *law), John Henry* **read** *law), Jno. Henry*
1257.8	647.37–8	**for** *Power eatondph 1/8* **read** *Power, .)eatondph 1/8*
1259.11	647.40	**for** *A., Edward J.* **read** *A., Edw. J.*
1260.4	647.40–41	**for** *Cornelius Kelleher,* **read** *Cornelius T. Kelleher,*
1262.6–7	647.43	**for** by *L. Boom* (as **read** by L. Boom (as

1273.8–9	648.14	**for** managing the thing, there. **read** managing to. There.
1277.1–2	648.18	**for** his sidevalue 1,000 **read** his side. Value 1,000
1277.10–11	648.19	**for** added for **read** added. For
1278.9, 1279.4	648.20–21	**for** by *Rightaway,* 5 yrs, 9st 4lbs, Thrale (W. **read** by *Rightaway– Thrale*, 5 yrs, 9st 4lbs, (W.
1284.11	648.26–7	**for** filly Sceptre on **read** filly *Sceptre* on
1285.5	648.27	**for** by Braine so **read** by Braime so
1295.10–11	648.39–40	**for** that, Mr Bloom said. **read** that, he, Bloom, said.
1311.4	649.15–16	**for** the stories and, **read** the stones and,
1333.5	649.42	**for** title *rôle* how **read** title role how
1337.6	650.4–5	**for** frigid expression notwithstanding **read** frigid exterior notwithstanding
1349.8	650.19–20	**for** course, Mr Bloom **read** course, as Bloom
1355.7–12	650.26	**for** her. I **read** her. She loosened many a man's thighs. I
1356.7	650.27	**for** barber's. Her husband **read** barber's. The husband
1368.3	650.42	**for** upon encouraging his **read** upon encompassing his
1378.4	651.11	**for** fact that the **read** fact the
1386.5	651.21	**for** folk? Though **read** folk? Poser. Though
1402.1	651.40	**for** And the coming **read** And then coming
1411.14–1412.5	652.10	**for** Stephen. And, **read** Stephen, about blood and the sun. And,

1423.8–10	652.22	**for** contents rapidly, **read** contents it contained rapidly,
1438.10–11	652.39	**for** about '96. Very **read** about ninety six. Very
1452.11–1454.5	653.12–13	**for** rest, yes, Puritanism. It does though, St. Joseph's sovereign ... whereas no **read** rest. Yes, puritanisme, it does though Saint Joseph's sovereign thievery alors (Bandez!) Figne toi trop. Whereas no
1491.2	654.14	**for** Proctor to **read** Proctor tries to
1495.7	654.19–20	**for** He, Bloom, enjoyed **read** He B, enjoyed
1496.12–1497.2	654.21–2	**for** occurred in the historic *fracas* when **read** occurred on the historic fracas when
1517.14–1518.2	655.4	**for** time, being **read** time all the same being
1530.4	655.18	**for** the cabmen and **read** the cabman and
1569.9–10	656.23	**for** eat, were **read** eat, even were
1575.1	656.29	**for** – Yesterday, exclaimed **read** – Yesterday! exclaimed
1585.10	656.42	**for** evicted tenants' question, **read** evicted tenants question
1586.9	656.43	**for** people's minds though, **read** people's mind though,
1592.5	657.7	**for** step further than **read** step farther than
1594.12–14	657.10	**for** fashion at **read** fashion by our friend at
1603.4	657.20	**for** weighing the **read** weighing up the
1636.5	658.17	**for** let XX equal **read** let X equal
1642.3	658.24–5	**for** or somewhere about in **read** or somewhereabouts in

1644.13	658.28	**for** come with **read** come home with
1652.10	658.37–8	**for** his (Bloom's) busy **read** his (B's) busy
1680.4	659.28	**for** *Arabian Nights' Entertainment* **read** *Arabian Nights Entertainment*
1682.1	659.30	**for** Thereupon he **read** Hereupon he
1692.3,5	659.41	**for** rise to his feet so **read** rise from his seat so
1699.8	660.7	**for** opposite to him **read** opposite him
1710.1	660.19	**for** down on **read** down, on
1710.6	660.19	**for** in cafes. **read** in cafés.
1714.5–8	660.23–4	**for** around nimbly, considering frankly, at **read** around, nimbly considering, frankly at
1715.15, 1716.1	660.25	**for** the by, the right **read** the bye, his right
1733.3	661.3	**for** they passed on **read** they turned on
1765.6	661.41	**for** whom Bloom did **read** whom B. did
1771.3	662.6	**for** the swing chain, a **read** the swingchains, a
1777.11	662.13–14	**for** perceiving Bloom **read** perceiving, Bloom
1778.9	662.14–15	**for** usual plucked **read** usual, plucked
1789.8–9	662.26–7	**for** big foolish nervous noodly **read** big nervous foolish noodly
1812.12–13	663.15	**for** of *Johannes Jeep* about **read** of Johannes Jeep about
1843.12–13	664.10–11	**for** time but **read** time. But
1859.9–10	664.29–30	**for** fellows and **read** fellows. And
1885.10–11	665.18–19	**for** indifferent. He merely **read** indifferent, but merely

1886.5–11	665.19–20	as he sat on his lowbacked car, **in italic, not roman**

17: Ithaca

28.6	666.33	**for** Bloom's view on **read** Bloom's views on
58.6	667.28–9	**for** Julius Mastiansky, **read** Julius (Juda) Mastiansky,
93.6	668.31–2	**for** Francis Frœdman, pharmaceutical **read** Francis Froedman, pharmaceutical
97.1	668.36	**for** sixtyfour, mohammedan era **read** sixtyfour, mohammadan era
111.1–5	669.17	**for** candle, a **read** candle of 1 C P, a
112.6	669.18–19	**for** candle of 1 C P. **read** candle.
141.3–148.2	670.15	**for** Island: of **read** Island: of his aunt Sara, wife of Richie (Richard) Goulding, in the kitchen of their lodgings at 62 Clanbrassil street: of
154.1	670.27–8	**for** with lisle suspender **read** with Lisle suspender
165.10	671.4	**for** of filter mains **read** of filtre mains
183.10	671.27	**for** watercarrier returning **read** watercarrier, returning
198.8–199.5	672.3	**for** peninsulas and **read** peninsulas and islands, its persistent formation of homothetic islands, peninsulas and
210.5–7	672.16	**for** by the **read** by the well by the
301.1	675.8	**for** eggcups, and open **read** eggcups, an open
302.2	675.9	**for** aromatic violet comfits. **read** aromatic (violet) comfits.

310.1	675.19	**for** one the **read** one, the
312.7	675.22	**for** a noggin and **read** a naggin and
318.1	675.28	**for** jamjars of **read** jamjars (empty) of
321.3–4	675.33	**for** 8 87, 8 86. **read** 8 87, 88 6.
391.4	677.34	**for** bearing on all **read** bearing in all
394.3	678.1	**for** prizes at 10/-, **read** prizes of 10/-,
394.9–10	678.1–2	**for** respectively by **read** respectively for competition by
411.5	678.19	**for** Marion Tweedy **read** Marion (Molly) Tweedy
423.5–11	678.35–6	**transfer** produced by R.Shelton 26 December 1892 **to 678.33 and read** *Sailor* (produced […] 1892, written […] Miss Whelan under the
443.3	679.17	**for** rhymes homophonous **read** rhymes, homophonous
479.2–3	680.20	**for** Riordan, a **read** Riordan (Dante), a
502.5–6	681.10	**for** round precipitous **read** round and round precipitous
517.5–8	681.28	**for** pleasant relaxation **read** pleasant rigidity, a more pleasant relaxation
522.2	681.33	**for** his table and **read** his stable and
535.1,4	682.10	**for** (subsequently Rudolf Bloom) of Szombathely, Vienna, **read** (subsequently Rudolph Bloom) of Szombathély, Vienna,
543.6	682.19	**for** Saint Nicolas Without, **read** Saint Nicholas Without,
553.9	682.32	**for** degree course of **read** degree courses of
565.9	683.8	**for** revolutionary for **read** revolutionary, for

603.11	684.12	**for** plumtree is a **read** plumtree in a
604.9	684.13–14	**for** Trumplee. Montpat. Plamtroo. **read** Trumplee. Moutpat. Plamtroo.
619.7–620.2	684.30–31	**for** Queen's hotel, Queen's hotel, Queen's Ho ... **read** Queen's Hotel, Queen's Hotel, Queen's Hotel. Queen's Ho ...
661.6	686.2–3	**for** tiddlywinks, spillikins, cup **read** tiddlywinks, spilikins, cup
712.4	687.22	**for** *More Neubkim* (Guide) **read** *More Nebukim* (Guide)
727.10	688.3	**for** *agus, suil* **read** *agus suil*
733.1–2	688.10	**insert, and begin the paragraph with,** By juxtaposition.
734.3	688.11	**for** style, entitled *Sweets* **read** style, entituled *Sweets*
739.4	688.16–17	**for** substituted goph, explaining **read** substituted qoph, explaining
759.7	689.1	**for** in Chanan David **read** in Chanah David
762.2	689.4	**for** ethnically irreductible consummation? **read** ethnically irreducible consummation?
793.3	690.7–8	**for** or Shakespearean exemplars, **read** or Shakespearean: exemplars,
808.1	690.19	**transfer the first block of musical notation to 691.4–5 following** *all.*
845.1	692.15	**for** the incitation of **read** the incitations of
873.10–874.3	693.12	**for** intervals to **read** intervals to more distant intervals to
909.8,13	694.17	**for** gifts 1) an owl, 2) a clock, given **read** gifts (1) an owl, 2) a clock), given

915.6–7	694.24	**for** positions clockwise of movable **read** positions of clockwise movable
926.4	694.37	**for** him not for her **read** him to her
936.4	695.8	**for** such extemporisation? **read** such an extemporisation?
952.3–5	695.26	**for** Dedalus, born Goulding, 26 **read** Dedalus (born Goulding), 26
958.5–6	695.34	**for** shillings, advanced **read** shillings sterling, advanced
981.4	696.26	**for** florin (2s.) with **read** florin (2/-) with
1006.1	697.16	**for** metamorphosis from **read** metamorphosis, from
1009.4	697.20	**for** in place **read** in the place
1024.1, 1027.1	698.1,3	**position** borne by [...] borne by **as separate lines, centred**
1030.7	698.7	**for** *exitu Israël de* **read** *exitu Israel de*
1043.1	698.22	**for** in incipent lunation, **read** in incipient lunation,
1047.1	698.26–7	**for** Canis Major) 10 **read** Canis Maior) 10
1053.6	698.34	**for** evermoving from **read** evermoving wanderers from
1083.5	699.33	**for** the problem of **read** the problems of
1099.1	700.13	**for** and all **read** and to all
1124.4	701.1	**for** but lesser **read** but of lesser
1145.3	701.21	**transfer** probable **to 701.25 in place of** future
1161.8	702.6	**for** rising, and **read** rising and
1171.9	702.18	**for** Stephen's gaze? **read** Stephen's, gaze?

1177.10	702.24	**for** invisible person, **read** invisible attractive person,
1194.4	703.5	**for** letter who **read** letter, who
1203.12	703.15–16	**for** circumcised (1st January, **read** circumcised (1 January,
1239.2–5	704.19–20	**transfer** Ned Lambert (in bed), **to precede** Tom Kernan (in bed),
1280.1	705.30	**for** furnitures? **read** furniture.
1310.3	706.29	**for** sustained, pedal, **read** sustained pedal,
1314.3	706.35	**for** and slender **read** and a slender
1331.1	707.17	**for** That truncated **read** The truncated
1356.10	708.9	**for** paternal creator. **read** paternal procreator.
1369.1–5	708.23–4	**insert additional entry** *The Beauties of Killarney* (wrappers).
1397.9	709.18	**for** by Eugene Sandow **read** by Eugen Sandow
1399.5–1406.8	709.21–31	**read** ſ **for** f **in** Engliſh Biſhop's epiſtle eſquire, requeſting perſon loft aftray, reftore Enniſcorthy, **and for the second** f **in** fineſt
1438.8	710.27	**for** black hair extending **read** black hairs extending
1516.3	712.38	**for** than 5 minutes **read** than 15 minutes
1521.7	713.4	**for** 2 servant's rooms, **read** 2 servants' rooms,
1534.7	713.20	**for** with a fingertame **read** with fingertame
1541.10	713.28	**for** tierod brace, **read** tierod and brace,
1543.2	713.30	**for** plain: servant's apartments **read** plain: servants' apartments

1556.8	714.3	**for** William, sweat pea, **read** William, sweet pea,
1557.11, 1558.2	714.5	**delete brackets enclosing** wholesale and retail
1558.6,8,9	714.5–6	**for** bulb merchant and nurseryman, agent for **read** bulb merchants and nurserymen, agents for
1599.6	715.16	**for** Indoor discussion **read** Indoor: discussion
1613.1–2	715.33–4	**for** L.L.D. *honoris causa*, Bloomville, **read** L.L.D. (*honoris causa*), Bloomville,
1619.9	716.4	**for** inequality of **read** inequality, of
1655.3	717.4	**for** 20,000, divided **read** 20,000 torchbearers, divided
1656.10	717.5	**for** and John **read** and (honest) John
1662.5	717.13	**for** 20 years purchase) **read** 20 years' purchase),
1679.9–10	717.33	**for** value: precious **read** value (precious
1680.8	717.34–5	**for** (7 shilling, mauve, **read** (7 schilling, mauve,
1683.7	717.38	**for** relic in **read** relic) in
1692.9–10	718.8	**for** delivery at **read** delivery per delivery at
1708.2	718.25	**for** to the census **read** to census
1723.9, 1724.6	719.3–4	**enclose** 10/– per […] (trilingual) included **in parentheses, not square brackets**
1733.4	719.14–15	**for** Lancashire Yorkshire **read** Lancashire and Yorkshire
1740.3–1741.2	719.23	**for** and for **read** and for Liverpool Underwriters' Association, the cost of acquired rolling stock for

177

1752.2	719.35	**for** What eventually would **read** What eventuality would
1761.6	720.8	**for** years passed **read** years are passed
1795.9–1796.8	721.10–11	**for** deceased: 3 **read** deceased: a cameo scarfpin, property of Rudolph Bloom (born Virag), deceased: 3
1799.10, 1800.1	721.14–15	**for** in reserved alphabetic boustrophedontic punctated **read** in reversed alphabetic boustrephodontic punctated
1806.9	721.22	**for** and faintruled notepaper, **read** and feintruled notepaper,
1815.11	721.33	**for** of measurements **read** of the measurements
1816.9	721.34	**for** 2 months of **read** 2 months' of
1821.9	721.40–41	**for** addressed to **read** addressed (erroneously) to
1822.9	721.41–2	**for** commencing: Dear **read** commencing (erroneously): Dear
1850.11	722.33	**for** the most immediate **read** the not immediate
1878.1	723.28	**for** ancient hagadah book **read** ancient haggadah book
1889.3–6	724.3	**for** man widower, unkempt hair, **read** man, widower, unkempt of hair,
1892.1	724.6–7	**for** septuagenarian suicide **read** septuagenarian, suicide
1901.1	724.16	**for** the tetragrammaron: the **read** the tetragrammaton: the
1909.9	724.27	**for** Maria Theresa, empress **read** Maria Theresia, empress

178

1939.7	725.25	**for** paying 1s. 4d. in **read** paying 1/4d in
1953.4	726.4	**for** nothing, or **read** nothing, nothing or
1964.11	726.17	**for** if now disunited **read** if not disunited
1984.8–9	727.3	**for** statues, nude **read** statues of nude
1993.12	727.14	**for** Ursa Major produced **read** Ursa Maior produced
1996.4	727.16–17	**for** Ursa Major. On **read** Ursa Maior. On
2001.2	727.23	**for** reward lost **read** reward, lost
2023.4	728.10	**for** or of the **read** or the
2047.1	728.38	**for** and Thummin): the **read** and Thummim): the
2071.10–2078.2	729.29–30	**for** walking, silently, **read** walking, charged with collected articles of recently disvested male wearing apparel, silently,
2078.5	729.36	**for** divinities, to **read** divinities: to
2079.8	729.37	**for** Mrs Bandman Palmer **read** Mrs Bandmann Palmer
2084.9	730.6–7	**for** by the hypothesis? **read** by hypothesis?
2118.13	731.8	**for** or adder: lightly, **read** or adders: lightly,
2142.5–6	731.35–6	**for** to nolast term. **read** to no last term.
2151.1	732.8	**for** transmitted first **read** transmitted, first
2164.6,8 2165.1	732.24–5	**for** Because action between agents and reagents at **read** Because attraction between agent(s) and reagent(s) at
2178.2	733.4	**for** As natural **read** As as natural
2181.12	733.8	**for** of collision **read** of a collision

179

2190.11	733.19	**for** other altered processes **read** other parallel processes
2203.7	733.35	**for** ocular witness), not **read** ocular witnesses), not
2205.5–2206.1	733.37	**for** impossibly. If **read** impossibly. Hushmoney by moral influence, possibly. If
2209.7	734.1–2	**for** protecting separator **read** protecting the separator
2210.12	734.4	**for** void incertitude, **read** void of incertitude,
2212.6	734.5	**for** hymen, the **read** hymen: the
2216.4	734.9	**for** female, the **read** female: the
2232.4–5	734.28–9	**for** adipose posterior **read** adipose anterior and posterior
2239.2	734.36	**for** revelation; a **read** revelation: a
2256.10	735.18	**for** Mrs Bandman Palmer **read** Mrs Bandmann Palmer
2259.9	735.21–2	**for** tendency entitled *Sweets* **read** tendency entituled *Sweets*
2260.4	735.22	**for** anonymous, author **read** anonymous author
2261.12	735.24	**for** of postcenal **read** of a postcenal
2289.9	736.21	**for** which in **read** which, in
2316.12	737.11	**for** depicted on a **read** depicted in a
2328.2	737.24	**for** to a dark **read** to dark

18: Penelope

4.4	738.4–5	**for** interesting to that **read** interesting for that
10.11	738.12	**for** wear I **read** wear them I
18.13	738.22	**for** them go **read** them to go
47.12	739.14	**for** room for the matches to **read** room to
54.1	739.22	**for** straws who **read** straws now who
62.5	739.32	**for** Christmas if **read** Christmas day if
67.13–14	739.39	**for** to bealone with **read** to be alone with
70.16	739.41–2	**for** saw too that **read** saw to that
70.14–71.11	739.41–3	**transfer** I saw to that **to 739.43 following** notice
83.8	740.15	**for** hes change **read** hes a change
127.10	741.26	**for** some liquor Id **read** some liqueur Id
129.8	741.28–9	**for** tasted one with **read** tasted once with
131.13	741.31	**for** time we **read** time after we
136.12–137.6	741.35	**transfer** as if the world was coming to an end **to 741.38 following** Gibraltar
135.9	741.36–7	**for** punish when **read** punish us when
137.8	741.38	**for** and they **read** and then they
143.8	742.2	**for** lamp yes because **read** lamp because
152.3	742.13	**for** us like **read** us or like
155.2	742.17	**for** pull it out **read** pull out
165.1	742.29	**for** your ear supposed **read** your ears supposed

173.12–13	742.39	**for** neck on **read** neck it was on
180.8	743.4–5	**for** the insides I **read** the inside I
183.4,7	743.8	**for** had on a coolness with **read** had a coolness on with
191.7	743.18	**for** well seen then **read** well see then
195.8–14	743.23	**transfer** to her **back in the same line, to follow** declaration
205.3	743.35	**for** me did **read** me and did
212.12	744.1	**for** falling one **read** falling out one
225.11	744.16–17	**for** Poldy anyway whatever **read** Poldy anyhow whatever
228.5	744.20	**for** like that and **read** like then and
229.5–6	744.21	**for** postcard up up **read** postcard U p up
236.1	744.29	**for** man yet it **read** man yes it
266.9	745.23	**for** street well and **read** street west and
306.13	746.29–30	**for** *Maria Santissima* he **read** *Maria Santisima* he
309.4	746.32	**for** with sunray **read** with the sunray
316.9	746.41	**for** out if it **read** out of it
332.7	747.5	**for** fool Henry Doyle **read** fool Henny Doyle
327.11–328.2	747.11–12	**for** writing a letter every morning sometimes **read** writing every morning a letter sometimes
354.3–4,6	747.43–748.1	**for** then he wouldnt believe next **read** then hed never believe the next
386.3	748.40	**for** man Griffith is **read** man Griffiths is
387.16	748.42	**for** of politics **read** of their politics

395.4	749.8	**for** the old **read** the other old
404.16	749.20	**for** gave theyve **read** gave him theyve
407.3	749.23	**for** going around with **read** going round with
419.16	749.38	**for** tingating either can **read** tingating cither can
456.7	750.40	**for** it thin **read** it the thin
485.10	751.32	**for** it all **read** it at all
486.13	751.33–4	**for** thing around her **read** thing round her
488.10	751.36	**for** Master François somebody **read** Master Francois somebody
492.1	751.40	**for** with the old **read** with that old
526.12–13	752.39	**for** trouble whats she there **read** trouble what shes there
544.11–559.11	753.25–43	**transfer** that disgusting [...] something there **to 753.18 following** cabbageleaf **and insert** about her **in 753.43 to precede** and that **so that the reconnected words read** asked him about her and that **(the references given here are to the lines as they stand on the pages of 1961)**
551.14	753.34	**for** eye or if **read** eye as if
559.9	753.43	**for** bang or something **read** bang of something
564.8	753.24–5	**for** has the nymphs **read** has nymphs
598.10	754.40–41	**for** old sweet sonnnng the **read** old sweeeetsonnnng the
601.9	755.1	**for** lying around hes **read** lying about hes
605.15, 606.4–5	755.6–7	**for** is the rain was lovely just **read** is that rain was lovely and refreshing just

610.12	755.12–13	**delete** the mosquito nets and
613.14	755.16	**for** on what she **read** on it she
614.12–13	755.17	**for** a P C to **read** a p c to
615.13	755.19	**for** a very clean **read** a *very* clean
619.12	755.24	**for** still theyre lovely **read** still there lovely
623.6,8	755.28	**for** affly xxxxx **read** affly Hester xxxxx
627.1	755.32	**for** ear clothes **read** ear these clothes
631.1	755.37	**for** the banderillos with **read** the banderilleros with
648.5–650.7	756.15	**following** change **insert** he was attractive to a girl in spite of his being a little bald intelligent looking disappointed and gay at the same time he was like Thomas in the shadow of Ashlydyat
660.1	756.27	**for** it this **read** it O this
661.6	756.28	**for** rolled up under **read** rolled under
667.2	756.35	**for** never come back **read** never came back
670.4,5	756.39	**for** the swell of the ship **read** the smell of ship
685.4–5	757.14	**for** old reveille **read** old bugles for reveille
697.8	757.28–9	**for** I supposed he **read** I suppose he
718.14	758.11	**for** now whatever possessed **read** now what possessed
719.4–5	758.12	**for** write after **read** write from Canada after
722.12	758.16	**for** always good humour well **read** always goodhumoured well
727.1	758.21	**for** acute pneumonia well **read** acute neumonia well

728.4–5	758.22	**for** mine its **read** mine poor Nancy its
730.2,9	758.24–5	**for** bereavement sympathy […] newphew with **read** bereavement symphathy […] newphew with
736.7	758.32	**for** Madrid silly **read** Madrid stuff silly
739.6	758.36	**for** all around you **read** all round you
743.15–744.2	758.41–2	**for** with precipit precipitancy with **read** with precipat precip itancy with
764.11	759.24	**for** passing I **read** passing but I
773.3	759.34	**for** engaged for fun **read** engaged for for fun
774.7	759.35	**for** believed that **read** believed me that
788.4	760.9	**for** open at the **read** open in the
804.9	760.29	**for** somewhere yes because **read** somewhere because
807.4	760.32	**for** never get far **read** never go far
808.12–809.2	760.34–5	**for** there all the time so tender how **read** there so tender all the time how
811.8	760.37–8	**for** petticoat I **read** petticoat because I
812.3	760.38	**for** I tortured the **read** I tormented the
813.5	760.39–40	**for** hotel rrrsssst awokwokawok **read** hotel rrrsssstt awokwokawok
814.14	760.41	**for** that morning I **read** that moaning I
819.15	761.4–5	**for** went around to **read** went round to
836.2	761.24	**for** his peaked cap **read** his peak cap
848.11	761.40	**for** along Willis road **read** along Williss road
856.5	762.6	**for** up windmill hill **read** up Windmill hill

869.14–15	762.22	**for** pearl must **read** pearl still it must
870.2–3	762.23	**for** pure 16 carat gold **read** pure 18 carrot gold
870.10–873.5	762.23	**following** very heavy **insert** but what could you get in a place like that the sandfrog shower from Africa and that derelict ship that came up the harbour Marie the Marie whatyoucallit no he hadnt a moustache that was Gardner yes
875.3–4	762.25–6	**for** days beyond recall close **read** days beyondre call close
877.4	762.28	**for** sweet ssooooooong Ill **read** sweet sooooooooooong Ill
899.1	763.11	**for** and vaulted rooms **read** and vaunted rooms
908.11	763.23	**for** more song **read** more tsong
925.4	763.43–764.1	**for** us Goodbye to **read** us goodbye to
930.10	764.7	**for** tea Findon **read** tea and Findon
939.1	764.17	**for** fresh plaice I **read** fresh place I
947.1	764.27	**for** pay and **read** pay it and
947.13	764.28	**for** and drive out **read** and drove out
955.5	764.37	**for** the boatmen he **read** the boatman he
958.2	764.40	**for** me to pull **read** me pull
959.2	764.42	**for** through through the **read** through the
966.13	765.8	**for** on you vomit **read** on youd vomit
977.6	765.20–1	**for** to go get **read** to to get
989.15	765.36	**for** day you never **read** day youd never
998.6	766.4	**for** off so **read** off him so

1007.4	766.14	**for** all at **read** all 1s at
1020.13– 1021.16	766.29–31	**transfer** and helping […] not him **to 766.32** **following** fact
1041.12	767.13	**for** pit at the pit at **read** pit at
1047.3	767.20	**for** me and **read** me yes and
1049.11	767.22	**for** mumps her **read** mumps and her
1057.8	767.32	**for** are few **read** are a few
1063.1	767.38	**for** lost always **read** lost shes always
1085.12	768.23	**for** the window **read** the area window
1092.9	768.30–31	**for** us wonder **read** us I wonder
1112.12	769.12	**for** him Drimmies **read** him in Drimmies
1124.11–16	769.26	**for** sheets the **read** sheets I just put on I suppose the
1148.5	770.12	**for** lily easy O **read** lily easy easy O
1158.14	770.25–6	**for** besides there something **read** besides theres something
1162.10	770.30	**for** my compriment I **read** my compriments I
1164.8	770.32	**for** he puts it **read** he put it
1179.9	771.8	**for** 4 or 5 **read** 4 and 5
1195.12	771.27	**for** day Id better **read** day I better
1196.1	771.28	**for** an all night sitting **read** an alnight sitting
1232.2	772.29	**for** hour wait **read** hour 1 wait
1251.1	773.9	**for** that we then I **read** that wethen I
1258.7	773.18–19	**for** top on his **read** top of his

1264.6	773.25–6	**for** L Bloom and **read** L Boom and
1290.3–7	774.14	**for** him and **read** him trotting off in his trowlers and
1295.2	774.19	**for** goodbye *sweet*heart **read** goodbye sweetheart *sweet*heart
1308.12–1309.12	774.36	**for** other of **read** other the first cry was enough for me I heard the deathwatch too ticking in the wall of
1324.17	775.11	**for** like Byron **read** like Lord Byron
1330.10	775.18	**for** and taking of **read** and talking of
1338.4	775.27	**for** I never go **read** I ever go
1352.10	776.2	**for** so simply I **read** so simple I
1354.5	776.4	**for** he looked with **read** he looks with
1382.10–11	776.37	**for** swelling upon you **read** swelling up on you
1392.8	777.6	**for** for stupid **read** for their stupid
1404.12	777.21	**for** ever I do **read** ever Id do
1405.14	777.22	**for** you señorita theres **read** you senorita theres
1412.19	777.31	**for** only to do **read** only do
1416.13	777.36	**for** ones old stockings **read** ones odd stockings
1464.10	779.8	**for** father Vial plana of **read** father Vilaplana of
1487.3	779.36	**for** estrellados señor Lord **read** estrellados senor Lord
1507.14	780.18	**for** fa pietà Masetto **read** fa pieta Masetto
1508.12	780.19	**for** son più forte **read** son piu forte

1515.14	780.28	**for** it in **read** it out in
1537.5	781.12	**for** it nor not **read** it or not
1543.13	781.20	**for** office the **read** office or the
1556.6	781.36	**for** of course a **read** of those a
1560.4	781.41	**for** with fields **read** with the fields
1595.3	782.40–41	**for** posadas glancing **read** posadas 2 glancing
1600.8	783.4	**for** and pink **read** and the pink

ALTERATIONS TO
1984

1 : Telemachus

Status Typescript (which is lost) probably copied from R

3.8   **for** him on the **read** him by the
                                LR and Egoist read 'on' – not in R or proofs

10.10   **for** surrounding land and **read** surrounding
                                country and
                                R reads 'land', but 'country' looks like a deliberate
                                emendation in TS, not a copying error

255.5   **for** fans, tasselled dancecards, **read** fans,
                                tasseled dancecards,
                                J wrote 'tasselled' in R, but 'tasseled' in aE

411.3   **for** could live **read** could only live
                                'only' not in R, probably a deliberate addition in TS

2 : Nestor

Status Typescript (which is almost all lost) probably copied from R

124.4   **for** His thick hair **read** His tangled hair
                                LR and Egoist read 'thick' (v. TN); retain R-1922
                                readings

139.7   **for** and thick hair **read** and tangled hair
                                LR and Egoist read 'thick' (v. TN); retain R-1922
                                readings

177.5   **for** his bench. **read** his desk.
                                R reads 'bench.'; 'desk.' is probably a deliberate
                                emendation in TS

246.12–13   **for** bay: it seems history **read** bay: history
                                LR and Egoist add 'it seems'; retain R-1922 reading

354.4   **for** said again, if **read** said, if
'again' could have been omitted in error by the typist, but
its omission was probably a deliberate emendation

3: Proteus

Status Typescript (which is almost all lost) probably copied from R

51.4   **for** long upon the **read** long on the
'upon' appears to be changed to 'on' in R (f. 2)

114.2   **for** *ne amplius decalveris.* **read** *ne nimium
decalveris.*
LR and Egoist read '*amplius*'; retain R-1922 reading

365.4   **for** me last **read** me up last
'up' is possibly a typist's error, but retained because it's an
addition, not a deletion or a substitution

374.8   **for** face hair **read** face her hair
'her' is possibly a typist's error, but retained because it's an
addition, not a deletion or a substitution

496.4   **for** one. This. Toothless **read** one. Toothless
'This.' deleted by J in placards (JJA 17 p. 59)

4: Calypso

Status HWG claims that TS (most of which is lost) was initially copied from R.
This was not Groden's view, neither is it ours, and we have proceeded on the
assumption that TS was copied from a lost working draft

* = TS (represented here by the printed tradition) followed in preference to
non-linear R

21.5   **for** kindly the **read** kindly, the
comma inserted, apparently by J, in page proofs (JJA 22
p. 219)

58.3   **for** She didn't want **read** She did not want*

133.4   **for** it you with **read** it with*

135.12   **for** more. Fifteen. **read** more. Ten. Fifteen.*

178.4   **for** duty cuddling her **read** duty cuddled her*

205.5   **for** still in **read** still alive in*

213.5   **for** them barefoot in **read** them in*

233.1–5   **delete** Yes, I am here now.*

273.6   **for** let the water **read** let water*

302.5   **for** were! she **read** were, she
                        R punctuation superseded by aE punctuation

399.4–5   **for** says I am quite **read** says I'm quite*

407.12–408.1   **for** swells and he **read** swells he*

413.7   **for** in hurry. **read** in a hurry*

418.2   **for** woman. Lot of **read** woman. Lots of*

421.5   **for** stared pityingly at **read** stared pitying at*

492.7   **for** has. Agendath what **read** has. Agenda
                        what*

498.8   **for** nextdoor windows. The **read** nextdoor
                        window. The*

5: Lotus Eaters

Status TS (which is lost) probably copied from a lost working draft, except for the beginning, which appears to have been copied from R ff.1–5a and which affects only the first emendation below

* = TS (represented here by the printed tradition) followed in preference to non-linear R

79.16–80.1	**for** letter the letter and **read** letter and HWG (TN) argues that the repetition is intentional, not a scribal error in R (f. 3); we disagree
259.1	**delete** x x x x *_*_ deleted by J in page proofs (JJA 22 p. 264)
296.8	**for** of a well, **read** of the well,*
323.7–8	**for** Claver S.J. and **read** Claver and*
347.5–13	**delete** Then the next one. Her hat sank at once.*
380.6	**for** Carey, yes. No, **read** Carey. No*
403.6	**for** music splendid. **read** music is splendid.*
404.4	**for** mass: *Gloria* **read** mass: the *Gloria**
404.10	**for** popes keen **read** popes were keen*
438.1	**for** in that Fermanagh **read** in the Fermanagh*
487.7	**for** inhaling slowly the **read** inhaling the*
505.11	**for** all the day. **read** all day.*

510.4   **for** of these soaps. **read** of those soaps.*

560.7   **for** Captain Culler broke **read** Captain Buller
                                   broke
                                   The MS addition (placards, JJA 17 p. 93) appears to read
                                   Buller, not Culler

6: Hades

Status TS (which is almost complete) probably copied from lost working draft

* = TS followed in preference to non-linear R

10.6   **for** it twice till **read** it tight till*

20.3   **for** envelope. Grows all **read** envelope. Grow
                                   all*

100.4–5   **for** thighs and eyed **read** thighs, eyed*

199.9–10   **for** reply: spruce figure: passed. **read** reply:
                                   passed.*

361.5   **for** Venetian blind. The **read** Venetian blinds.
                                   The*

361.8   **for** coroner's sunlit ears, **read** coroner's ears,*

394.14   **for** quarter lost: **read** quarter is lost:*

473.5   **for** Cunningham added. That's **read**
                                   Cunningham said. That's*

509.10   **new paragraph at** Coffin now.
                                   new paragraph probably intended (placards, JJA 17 p.
                                   240)

609.5	**for** Mervyn Browne. Down **read** Mervyn Brown. Down:*
612.6	**for** a doner. **read** a goner. ‘doner’ in R and TS, but J changed it to ‘goner’ in page proof (JJA 22 p. 416)
638.14	**for** the trundled barrow **read** the barrow*
662.2	**for** secretsearching. Mason **read** secretsearching eyes. Mason*
693.4	**for** said, Madame Marion **read** said, Madam Marion*
747.1	**for** Wonder he **read** Wonder how he*
779.9	**for** black, black treacle **read** black, treacle*
865.8	**for** turned away his **read** turned his*
918.2–3	**for** staying at whiles to **read** staying awhile to*
950.7	**for** us. Hoo! Not **read** us. Hu! Not*

7: Aeolus

Status TS probably copied from lost working draft

* = TS followed in preference to non-linear R

70.4	**for** through a sidedoor **read** through the sidedoor*
118.9	**for** *Freeman's Journal* office. **read** *Freeman's Journal.**
168.8–10	**for** symmetry with a y of **read** symmetry of*

171.2   **for** I should have **read** I could have*

219.10   **for** Number? Yes. Same **read** Number?
               Same*

223.1   **for** over those walls **read** over these walls*

270.6   **for** of Cicero, professor **read** of Cicero's,
               professor*

305.7   **for** show the grey **read** show their grey
               'their' is J's final version in proof (placards, JJA 18 pp. 9,
               19)

328.2   **for** *moon shine forth* **read** *moon shines forth**

350.1   **for** – Getonouthat, you **read** – Getououthat,
               you*

532.9   **for** and I knew **read** and knew*

557.3   **for** domination. *Domine!* Lord! **read**
               domination. *Dominus.* Lord!*

600.8   **for** the Bastile, J.J. **read** the Bastille, J.J.
               not an acceptable spelling for *the* Bastille (despite HWG's
               reference to OED, which gives 'Bastile' for *a* Bastile only);
               therefore accept scribal correction to TS

648.14   **for** is it? **read** is he?*

672.12   **for** is Davy's publichouse, **read** is Burke's
               publichouse,
               three lines up (669.4) J changed 'Burke's' to 'Davy's' in
               TS, but did not make the change here (JJA 12 p. 296);
               since the contradiction may have been intended to indicate
               the crazed nature of Crawford's mind, reject HWG's
               emendation

708.4   **for** nonsense. Psha! Only **read** nonsense.
               Only*

722.1   **for** *oriafiamma,* gold **read** *oriafiamma,* in gold*

735.4   **for** *The Skibbereen Eagle.* **read** *The Skibereen Eagle.*
both spellings are used, and J wrote one 'b' in proof (placards, JJA 18 p. 61; cf. 16–666 below)

802.7–14   **for** thing, Myles Crawford said, in a child's frock. **read** thing in a child's frock, Myles Crawford said.*

817.8–9   **for** loose white silk neckcloth **read** loose neckcloth*

870.8   **for** enjoying a silence. **read** enjoying silence.*

875.3   **for** Lenehan added. And **read** Lenehan said. And*

890.10   **for** All that are **read** All who are*

899.9   **for** cried, clapping Stephen **read** cried, slapping Stephen*

928.1   **for** Face glistering tallow **read** Face glistening tallow*

933.7   **for** and sixpences and **read** and a sixpence and*

955.10   **for** steps, scattering in **read** steps, scampering in*

975.2   **for** it copied if **read** it if*

1072.5   **for** said smiling grimly. **read** said grimly.*

8: Lestrygonians

Status TS probably copied from lost working draft

* = TS followed in preference to non-linear R

123.5   **for** whitesmocked sandwichmen marched **read** whitesmocked men marched
'sandwichmen' in LR only

146.9   **for** of a woman **read** of woman*

149.5   **for** knew I, I **read** knew, I
scribal amendment to TS (JJA 12 p. 306)

393.4–9   **for** look all of a sudden after. **read** look after all of a sudden!*

394.1   **for** their mind. Old **read** their minds. Old*

409.11   **for** up in groups **read** up into groups*

463.13   **for** mob. Or gas **read** mob. Want to gas*

497.4–7   **delete** Like a mortuary chapel.*

506.8   **for** Charley Kavanagh used **read** Charley Boulger used
'Kavanagh' in LR only

569.1–6   **delete** Looking up from the back garden.*

580.4–7   **for** fell to his side again. **read** fell again to his side.*

594.2–3   **for** With ha quiet keep quiet relief **read** With a keep quiet relief
scribal amendment to TS (JJA 12 p. 312)

594.13   **for** is the street **read** is street*

595.5   **for** day of Bob **read** day Bob*

598.4   **for** year sober **read** year as sober*

623.2–5   **for** here. *Lacaus esant tara tara.* Great **read** *La causa è santa!* Great
amendment to placards (JJA 18 p.112); cf. 13–862, 15–2385

623.9–10   **for** that. *Taree tara.* Must **read** that. Tara. Must
TS plus amendments in proof (TS, JJA 12 p. 313; placards, JJA 18 p. 112)

625.10   **for** one. Sticking them **read** one. Stick them*
also scribal amendment to TS (JJA 12 p. 313)

651.7   **for** meatjuice, slush of **read** meatjuice, slop of
'slush' in LR only

660.3   **for** gristle: gums: no **read** gristle: no
'gums:' in LR only

672.1–3   **transfer paragraph** His gorge rose. **to** 670.3 **and read** men. His gorge rose. Spaton
confirmed by placards (JJA 18 p. 123)

687.10   **for** the head bailiff, **read** the bailiff,*

721.7   **for** stinks after Italian **read** stinks Italian*

725.5   **for** buckets wobbly lights. **read** buckets wobble lights.*

867.4   **for** he oysters old **read** he oyster old*

868.12–14   **for** like things high. Tainted **read** like tainted*

908.6–8   **for** mumbled sweetsour of her spittle. **read**
                     mumbled sweet and sour with spittle.*

928.6   **for** of women sculped **read** of woman sculped*

931.12–932.1   **for** something drop. See **read** something fall
                     see*

962.12–963.3   **delete** He's an excellent brother.*

983.11   **for** up. He's been **read** up. He has been*

989.10–990.1   **for** followed frowning, a **read** followed, a*

1108.9   **for** their forehead perhaps: **read** their
                     foreheads perhaps:*

1119.8   **for** buy for Molly's **read** buy Molly's*

1128.2   **for** voice, temperatures: when **read** voice,
                     temperature: when*

1140.10   **for** between his waistcoat **read** between
                     waistcoat*

1172.8   **for** walk. Not see. Get **read** walk. Not see.
                     Not see. Get*

1173.9   **for** windy steps he **read** windy strides he*

1185.2   **for** looking. **read** looking for.*

1186.4   **for** back quick Agendath. **read** back quickly
                     Agendath.*

1189.7–9   **for** Trousers. Potato. Purse. Where? **read**
                     Trousers. Purse. Potato. Where did I?*

1192.10–12   **for** there I yes. **read** there! Yes
scribal amendment in TS (JJA 12 p. 322)

9: Scylla and Charybdis

Status TS probably copied from lost working draft

* = TS followed in preference to non-linear R

132.2   **for** his palms. Nine **read** his palm. Nine*

427.1–431.1   **delete** – Will he not see reborn in her, with the memory of his own youth added, another image?
Do you know what you are talking about?
Love, yes. Word known to all men. *Amor vero aliquid alicui bonum vult unde et ea quae concupiscimus* ...*

435.8   **for** or to repeat **read** or repeat*

450.7   **for** There's a **read** There is a*

455.4   **for** and he had **read** and had*

482.2   **for** Amen! was responded **read** Amen! responded*

592.7   **for** off, out. **read** off and out.*

599.3–4   **for** *Guardian*. Last year. 1903. **read** *Guardian*. 1903.*

644.7   **for** for any cockcanary. **read** for every cockcanary.*

679.9   **new paragraph at** O, yes,*

684.5	**new paragraph at** You mean*
685.1–2	**for** But that has **read** That has*
726.8–727.1	*A quart of ale is a dish for a king.* **in roman not italic***
803.10–11	**for** stayed with her at **read** stayed at*
804.8	**for** town council paid **read** town paid*
814.9	**for** wife or father? **read** wife and father?*
855.10	**for** a new male: **read** a male:*
925.2–3	**for** coat and crest he **read** coat of arms he*
999.4	**for** poor are not, **read** poor is not,*
1008.7–8	**for** Maynooth. An **read** Maynooth – an*
1108.12–1109.3	**for** After. His lub back: I **read** After his lub back I*
1112.4	**for** no thought. **read** no thoughts.*

10: Wandering Rocks

Status TS copied from R, of which ff. 1–31 (lines 1–955) are in J's hand and ff.32–48 (lines 956–1282) are in Budgen's hand

536.4	**for** a long spread **read** a big spread HWG misreads R (f.17), which has 'big'
547.13	**for** and curaçoa to **read** and curacoa to misreading of TS (JJA 13 p. 17), in which the 'c' is not apparently marked with a cedilla

634.9   **for** rudely, puked phlegm **read** rudely, spat
phlegm
overwritten in R (f. 20), and postdates typing (v. TN);
reject because non-linear

691.12   **for** bell but **read** bell: but
there is a colon in both R (f. 22) and TS (JJA 13 p. 20)

714.3–4   **for** mouth gently: **read** mouth:
dropped in TS (JJA 13 p. 20), to which J adds a colon
without reinstating the word

984.3   **for** la maison Claire **read** la Maison Claire
J wrote M in R (f. 33); unnecessary normalisation by
HWG

995.2, 997.5, 1017.5,   **for** long *in* long John Fanning **read** Long
102.18, 1026.14, 1027.4

J was inconsistent, but markedly preferred 'Long' to 'long';
worth normalising here (as in 1922) as a concentrated
group

1177.2   **for** lieutenantcolonel Heseltine, drove **read**
lieutenantcolonel Hesseltine, drove
J (here and at 10–1222 below) clearly preferred '-ss-' to
'-s-', and inserted the extra 's' in TS (JJA 13 p. 29); reject
TN

1191.6   **for** the costbag of **read** the costsbag of
R (f. 44) reads 'costsbag' – reject harmonisation with
10–472

1215.1   **for** Anderson's alltimesticking watches **read**
Anderson's all times ticking watches
marked for separation in page proof (JJA 24 p. 153)

1222.10   **for** H.G.Heseltine, and **read** H.G.Hesseltine,
and
see 10–1177 above, and page proof (JJA 24 p. 137)

1259.1   **for** H.Shrift, T.M. **read** H.Thrift, T.M.
HWG misreads Budgen's 'Th' (R f.47; cf. his 'They' at R
f.36, line 9 up)

1277.9   **for** and Lansdowne roads **read** and
Landsdowne roads
HWG's unnecessary emendation

11: Sirens

Status TS probably copied from lost working draft

* = TS followed in preference to non-linear R

8.6   **for** satiny breast of **read** satiny breasts of*

13.5–6   **for** look: the **read** look! The*

13.9, 14.1–3   **transfer** O rose! **to 13.9 following** stars fade.
and no new segment at Castile. The **which
follows** chirruping answer.*

28.1   **for** Clapclap. Clipclap. **read** Clapclop.
Clipclap.*

39.2   **new segment at** Deepsounding. Do*

43.1   **for** *Naminedamine.* **read** Naminedamine.*

43.2–4, 44.1   **delete** Preacher is he. **and no new segment
at** All gone. **which follows** Naminedamine.*

64.4,8   **for** miss Douce ... miss Kennedy ... **read**
Miss Douce ... Miss Kennedy ... **and so
throughout the episode (40 further
occurrences)***

100.3   **for** thnthnthn, bootssnout sniffed **read**
thnthnthn, bootsnout sniffed*

126.5   **for** now a fulldrawn **read** now fulldrawn*

162.3–4   **for** sighing, sighing, **read** sighing. Sighing,*

164.4   **for** bending over **read** bending again over*

174.5–8   **for** laughter, after, gold after bronze, they **read** laughter, after bronze in gold, they*

180.5   **for** to greaseabloom. **read** to greaseaseabloom.*

187.9–10   **for** him for that par. **read** him about Keyes's par.*

224.2   **for** None nought said **read** None not said*

286.14–15   **for** the bar and diningroom **read** the diningroom*

303.2   **for** is. Again. Third **read** Is. Third*

349.1   **for** Smart Boylan bespoke **read** Boylan bespoke*

352.5–8   **for** four she. Who said four? **read** four he. All said four.*

353.5   **for** and bulging apple **read** and Adam's apple*

365.5   **for** her oblique jar **read** her jar*

413.3   **for** She set free **read** She let free*

419.13–420.1   **for** his chalice tiny, sucking **read** his tiny chalice, sucking*
confirmed by tE

421.1   **for** went after, after her **read** went after her*

459.1–3   *Love and War,* **in roman, not italic**
                   HWG's emendation, to harmonise with italicised *Love and
                   War* at 11–553 (which itself is not underlined in TS, JJA
                   13 p. 67)

500.2–3   **for** Marion. Met **read** Marion met*
                   confirmed by aE

546.6–7   **for** she need not trouble. **read** she needn't
                   trouble.*

553.8–10   *Love and War* **in roman, not italic***
                   see 11–459, above

563.9–11   **for** moist (a lady's) hand **read** moist, a lady's,
                   hand*

568.1   **delete** Jingle.*

606.9   **for** elephant jingly jogged. **read** elephant
                   jingle jogged.*

610.9   **for** said: *Sonnambula.* He **read** said:
                   Sonambula. He
                   1932 emendation; R (f. 21) and TS (JJA 13 p. 68) both
                   read *Sonambula*

639.10–640.1   **transfer** Still hold her back. **to 639.4**
                   following the moon.*

701.5–6   **for** swelling, full **read** swelling. Full*

705.5   **for** warm jamjam lickitup **read** warm jimjam
                   lickitup*

710.4–5   **for** *hope is* ... **read** *hope* ...*

738.9   **for** must martha feel. **read** must Martha feel.
                   scribal emendation in page proof (JJA 24 p. 224)

757.1–2	**for** Clapclipclap clap. Sound **read** Clapclipclap. Sound*
759.2–3	**for** Mina Kennedy, two **read** Mina, two*
782.12–13	**for** voice *lives not* ask **read** voice ask*
792.2	**for** all others. **read** all the others.*
793.12	**for** silence after you **read** silence you*
865.10	**for** ee. Accep my **read** ee. Accept my*
865.13	**for** poor litt pres **read** poor little pres*
870.6	**for** the string of **read** the pin of*
901.9	**for** read. There. Right. **read** read. Right.*
929.2	**for** did, faith, sir **read** did, sir*
942.12	**for** Turks the mouth, **read** Turks their mouth,*
943.6–7	**for** sheet. Yashmak. **read** sheet, a yashmak*
954.10	**for** her tankards waiting. **read** her tankard waiting*
961.6–7	**for** One: one, one, one, one, one: two, **read** One: one, one, one: two,*
984.4–7	**for** Diddleiddle addleaddle ooddleooddle. Hissss. Now. **read** Diddle iddle addle addle oodle oodle. Hiss. Now.*
1017.5–9	**delete** With bows a traitor servant.*

1021.11   **for** his footsteps there, **read** his footstep
                     there,*

1079.8   **for** Chickabiddy's owny Mumpsypum. **read**
                     Chickabiddy's own Mumpsypum.*

1091.7–11   **delete** Say something. Make her hear.*

1115.5   **for** passed, reposed and, **read** passed, repassed
                     and,*

1127.1   **transfer** Ow. **to follow** Bloom stood up.
                     correctly placed in 1922 (v. page proof, JJA 24 p. 268)

1143.3   **for** heard the growls **read** heard growls*

1146.6   **for** Dedalus cried. By **read** Dedalus said. By*

1176.3–4   **for** Mina. Mr Dollard. And **read** Mina. And*

1225.8–9   **for** house. Counted them. Litigation. **read**
                     house. Litigation.*

1241.4–6   **for** pipe. Pwee little wee. Policeman **read**
                     pipe. Policeman*

1255.2–3   **for** Heehaw shesaw. **read** Heehaw. Shesaw.
                     1922 probably correct (v. placards, JJA 19 p. 88)

1258.1–2   **for** made knowing **read** made. Knowing
                     J's correction on placards (JJA 19 p. 88)

1263.1   **for** envisaged battered candlesticks **read**
                     envisaged candlesticks*

12: Cyclops

Status TS copied from R

1025.1	**for** eye, adrinking fizz **read** eye, drinking fizz dubious pencil emendation in R f.33 – probably a non-linear change, post-dating the typing
1163.7–8	**for** citizen, that's what's the **read** citizen, that was the R f.37 reads 'that was', successive changes up to 1932; prefer the original form
1681.7	**for** Brigittines, Premonstratensians, Servi, **read** Brigittines, Premonstratesians, Servi, although peculiar, –esi–, not –ensi–, is J's own spelling

13: Nausicaa

Status TS probably copied (for the most part) from lost working draft

* = TS followed in preference to non-linear R

24.6	**for** over to him **read** over him*
33.14	**for** baby Boardman was **read** baby was*
56.1	**for** was too after **read** was after*
77.1	**for** where the gentleman couldn't **read** where gentlemen couldn't*
130.14–131.3	**delete** off the London bridge road*
133.12–13	**for** to go to Trinity **read** to Trinity*
145.10–13	**for** size too he and she and **read** size and*

157.14–15   **for** bow of silk to **read** bow to*

167.14   **for** buckle over her **read** buckle at her
J wrote 'over' on TS (JJA 13 p. 274) and 'at' on placards
(JJA 19 p. 241); prefer the later reading

180.7   **for** and lucky too **read** and the lucky colour
too*

185.8   **for** lovers' meeting if **read** lovers' meetings if*

186.2–12   **delete** or if they got untied that he was
thinking about you*

194.13   **for** the very first **read** the first*

201.7   **for** in Stoer's (he **read** in Stoers' (he*

221.7   **for** Edy, little spitfire, **read** Edy, the spitfire,*

276.1   **for** forget her the **read** forget the*

304.6   **for** Gerty, rapt in **read** Gerty, wrapt* in
worth keeping the TS reading (JJA 13 p. 277), which may
be a deliberate pun

328.1   **for** rubbed the **read** rubbed on the*

329.2   **for** her mother's taking **read** her mother
taking*

377.6   **for** father Father Hughes **read** father Hughes*

382.9   **for** Cissy Caffrey played **read** Cissy played*

498.4   **for** sing the *Tantum* **read** sing *Tantum*
'the' comes from the first rough draft, and is not in R or
TS

535.5 **for** I'll run ask **read** I'll ask
LR adds 'run' – retain R-1922 reading

539.3 **for** looking up at **read** looking at*

544.9 **for** mind please telling **read** mind telling*

569.9 **for** had had the **read** had the*

649.2–4 **for** tears for she felt that **read** tears that*

675.1–2 **for** tabernacle and genuflected and **read** tabernacle and*

700.10 **for** knew too about **read** knew about*

717.6–7 **for** and they all shouted **read** and shouted*

718.13 **for** flying through **read** flying about through*

783.13 **for** with the same **read** with same*

891.11 **for** home. Featherbed **read** home the Featherbed*

934.9–10 **for** Tommy and Jacky ran **read** Tommy ran*

945.11 **for** my name and **read** my and*

947.5 **for** *was Jemina Brown* **read** *was Jemima Brown**
HWG misreads R f.45 (the same error occurs independently in 1926–61)

968.12 **for** them. It's the **read** the. It is the*

1021.7 **for** anything, like rainbow **read** anything, rainbow*

1031.5–6	**for** women, instance, warn **read** women for instance warn*
1034.13	**for** gloves long John **read** gloves Long John*
1035.7–8	**for** other day. Breath? **read** other. Breath?*
1069.9	**for** Grace Darling. People **read** Grace darling. People J wrote 'darling' (placards, JJA 19 p. 301; cf. 13–1280) – keep it
1071.2	**for** better. Women. Light **read** better. Light*
1102.7,10–11	**for** me. Never again. My youth. Only **read** me. My youth. Never again. Only*
1145.12–13	**for** out. Or what **read** out what*
1161.6	**for** lifebelt round him, **read** lifebelt round round him,*
1164.11–1165.1	**for** down so peaceful. Not **read** down. Not*
1166.2–3	**for** A last lonely candle **read** A lost long candle*
1208.6,8	**for** a rich gentleman coming with **read** a* gentleman with*
1214.13	**for** of Keyes, museum **read** of keys, museum*
1281.7	**for** Raoul de perfume **read** Raoul to perfume J's correction on TS (JJA 13 p. 293) supersedes R
1283.8	**for** years of dreams **read** years dreams*
1299.6	**for** canarybird that **read** canarybird bird that J inserted 'canarybird' very carefully in TS (JJA 13 p. 293), and probably retained 'bird' deliberately

14: Oxen of the Sun

Status TS probably copied (for the most part) from lost working draft

* = TS followed in preference to non-linear R

20.6	**for** there unilluminated as **read** there inilluminated as*
54.1	**for** so hoving itself, **read** so having itself,* 'hoving' is an attractive reading, but TS (JJA 14 p. 172) overrides it
76.7	**for** Watchers tway there **read** Watchers twey there*
82.9	**for** she drad that **read** she dread that*
111.6–7	**for** come in to the **read** come into the*
117.7–8	**for** it all forth to **read** it forth all to*
117.11–118.1	**delete** for because she knew the man*
120.13	**for** a fair face **read** a young face*
132.4–5	**for** go in to that **read** go into that*
134.6	**for** a subtile. Also **read** a subtle. Also*
145.7	**for** fix then in **read** fix in*
148.3–5	**for** he blases in to them **read** he blares into them* HWG refers to OED 'blaze' v², but OED 'blare' v⁴ is equally relevant; TS (JJA 14 p. 173) preferred
156.12–13	**for** do in to it **read** do into it*

165.5	**for** of this wile. **read** of his wile.*
219.7–8	**for** and said **read** and when he said*
241.2	**for** Then spake young **read** Then spoke young*
250.5	**for** to bear beastly **read** to bring forth beastly*
286.6	**for** and goldsmith notes **read** and goldsmiths' notes*
315.11	**for** did straightways now **read** did now*
317.1, 318.1	**delete dialogue dash and separate paragraph, and run on 317.1–9 between 316.1 and 318.1***
325.11–12	**for** and shaked him with **read** and with*
326.6	**for** whiles they all **read** whiles all*
328.1	**for** in peasestraw, **read** in the peasestraw,*
368.11	**for** and broughtedst in **read** and broughtest in*
370.7	**for** against my light **read** against the light*
374.2	**for** and to the **read** and the*
388.5	**for** things accord in **read** thing accords in*
394.4	**for** from waters of **read** from water of*
405.1	**delete dialogue dash***

412,12   **for** waxed wan as **read** waxed pale as*

424.11   **for** the braggart's side **read** the braggart' **side***

437.10   **for** plugged him up **read** plugged up*

472.4   **for** arm up and **read** arm and*

491.12   **for** water flowing that **read** water running that*

506.1   **for** of Mercy's, Vin. **read** of Mercy, Vin.*

507.1–3   **for** sad about a racer he **read** sad for a racinghorse he*

561.7   **for** to hoof it **read** to foot it
                         a suspect and unnecessary reading from 1926 – reject

563.3   **for** choking chicken behind **read** choking chickens behind*

570.3   **for** wether wool, having **read** wether wools, having*

616.10   **for** out he'd run **read** out he run*

636.17   **for** it upon what **read** it up on what*

667.4   **for** expatiating upon his **read** expatiating **on** his*

674.8   **for** prey to the **read** prey for the*

714.2   **for** of person, **read** of his person,*

718.4   **for** had late befallen **read** had befallen*

724.12   **for** poor body, from **read** poor lady, from*

734.12   **for** the storm of **read** the storms of*

759.1–2   **for** me prettily) in **read** me) in*

771.8–11   **delete** he exclaimed in anguish.*

772.7   **for** had but remembered **read** had
                                    remembered*

813.9   **for** and with immodest **read** and immodest*

846.11   **for** with as being **read** with being*

856.1   **for** crookback toothed and **read** crookback
                                    teethed and*

857.11   **for** as to put **read** as it put*

861.10   **for** of rare **read** of a rare*

930.1   **for** of the ploughshare? **read** of a
                                    ploughshare?*

943.2   **for** ceremonial usage of **read** ceremonial
                                    usages of*

951.5   **for** and obstetrician rendered **read** and officer
                                    rendered*

953.7   **for** to refrain. The **read** to restrain. The*

954.11   **for** only bond of **read** only band of
                                    'bond' is from an early draft – R (f. 41) and TS (JJA 14 p.
                                    187) agree on 'band'

962.3–5   **for** simulated or dissimulated, the acardiac **read** simulated and dissimulated, acardiac*

962.9–10   **for** *foetu* and aprosopia **read** *foetu*, aprosopia*

971.8   **for** the perpetration of **read** the perpetuation of
prefer 1926 errata reading – reject TN

974.2   **for** of multiseminal, twikindled **read** of multigeminal, twikindled:*

986.8   **for** of those swineheaded **read** of swineheaded*

1002.7   **for** dilemma created in **read** dilemma in*

1015.6   **for** a ghostly grin. **read** a ghastly grin.*

1043.5–11   **delete** A score of years are blown away.*

1044.1–3   **for** Leopold. There, as **read** Leopold, as*

1106.6   **for** of the cold **read** of cold*

1121.1–5   **for** meditate, to acclaim you Stephaneforos. I **read** meditate. I*

1159.14   **for** in that little **read** in the little*

1193.12–14   **for** of the neck of the **read** of the*

1245.11   **for** he alleged, and **read** he alleges, and*

1305.2   **for** (an esthete's allusion, **read** (an esthetic allusion,*

1390.7

for the word. **read** the Word.*
TS appears to read cap 'W' (JJA 14 p. 194), not high 'w';
but this is not certain

1408.2

for celestial, glistening on **read** celestial,
glistering on*

1444.1

for Forward to the **read** Forward the*

1448.13

for samee dis bunch. **read** samee this bunch.*

1454.2

for Beatitudes! *Retamplatan digidi* **read**
Beatitudes! *Retamplan digidi*

1460.10–11

for high. Beer, beef, trample **read** high.
Beerbeef trample*

1492.10

for of peppe, you **read** of pepper you*

1505.13

for nae tha fou. **read** nae the fou.
J wrote 'the' here in R (f. 63), also in TS (JJA 14 p. 197)
as an addition for 14–1565, and seems to have meant it –
reject 1932 emendation

1533.2

for Right. Boniface! **read** Right Boniface!
by inserting this stop (which is not apparently intended, v.
TS, JJA 14 p. 197) HWG obscures the command '*Right
Boniface!*'

1539.13–1540.6

for bungellow kee tu find plais whear tu lay
read bungalo kee to find plais whear to lay*

1544.8–9

for Time gents! Who **read** Time. Who*

1556.6

for cos fren Padney **read** cos frien Padney*

1565.5

for nae tha fou **read** nae the fou
J wrote 'the' on TS (JJA 14 p. 197) – see 14–1505 above

15: Circe

Status TS copied (for the most part) from R, either directly or, from f.45, via an amanuensis copy

10.2, 12.2	**for** THE CALL [...] THE ANSWER **read** THE CALLS [...] THE ANSWERS we read these words in R f.1 as plurals, not singulars, and reject TN
409.4–6	**for** servants in livery too if **read** servants too in livery if the two versions inserted separately by J on two copies of the TS (JJA 15 pp. 18, 170); prefer the transmitted version
649.1–2–650.4–5	**separate and position** (*He gazes* [...] *phallic design.*) **as a narrative direction** R f.16 clearly indicates a narrative direction here
829.6	**for** *meekness glum*) That **read** *meekness*) That the word read as 'glum' is illegible in R f.20, but is probably an erasure
922.2–923.1	**end the first narrative direction at** *bargain ever ....*) **and begin a separate narrative direction at** (*Renewed laughter.* in this and the next entry, follow R ff.21–2 in separating the narrative directions into two parts, the first part in each case paraphrasing Bloom's speeches and the second part describing the situation
934.10–935.1	**end the first narrative direction at** *back number.*) **and begin a separate narrative direction at** (*Uproar and* see 15–922 above
1356.9	**for** Walter Ralegh brought **read** Walter Raleigh brought scribal 'i' added to page proof (JJA 26 p. 124)
1766.4–5	**for** *bread, sheep's tails,* **read** *bread, sheeps' tails,* J clearly wrote 'sheeps'' (R app. f.5), even though it's wrong – reject HWG's emendation

1908.3 **for** *(George R Mesias,* **read** *(George S Mesias,*
J wrote 'S' (R app. f.7) – reject HWG's emendation

2093.3 **for** the alrightness of **read** the alrightiness of
R f.34 is ambiguous here, but prefer TS 'alrightiness'

2097.6 **for** *spleen*) Ba! It **read** *spleen*) Bah! It
in this and the next two entries, HWG removes the 'h'
from 'Bah!' to harmonise with 'Ba!' at 15–114; but J wrote
'Bah!' in all three places here, 'Ba!' there

2098.11 **for** life. Ba! **read** life. Bah!
see 15–2097 above

2103.1 **for** Ba! **read** Bah!
see 15–2097 above

2163.7 **for** *Rien va plus!* **read** *Rien n'va plus!*
J wrote *'va'* in R (f. 36); the more 'correct' *'n'va'* is from
TS (JJA 15 p. 216)

3594.4–5 **for** that? The distrait or **read** that? *Le distrait*
or
Amanuensis MS (JJA 14 p. 329) appears to have 'Le'
written over 'The'

3812.10–3813.1 **for** Weeshwashtkissinapooisthnapoohuck?
read Weeshwashtkissinapooisthnapoohuck!
reject '?' on R f.62a (v. TN) – the mark there is exactly
like the '!' following 'kisses' 12 lines up

3838.5 **for** *and Tunney's tawny* **read** *and Tunny's
tawny*
HWG's normalisation – J wrote 'Tunny's' here

3982.11–3983.1 **for** *nag on spavined whitegaitered* **read** *nag,
stumbling on whitegaitered*
the typist could not read *'on spavined'* (R f. 66) and left it
out (JJA 15 pp. 129–30); J wrote the later version as a
correction to placards (JJA 20 p. 198)

4043.4   **for** or Levenston's. Fancy **read** or
Levinstone's. Fancy
'Levenston's' is HWG's normalisation to harmonise with
8–1139 – J wrote 'Levinstone's' here

4381.13   **for** do, you **read** do – you
the dash is J's later thought (placards, JJA 20 p. 213) –
prefer it

4452.7   **for** *Lincoln's Inn bencher* **read** *Lincoln's Inns'
bencher*
J wrote 'Inns'' on the amanuensis copy (JJA 14 p. 362);
reject emendation of 1926

16: Eumaeus

Status TS copied from R

+ = R followed in preference to the primitive draft (HWG's 'P'), from which R
was expanded and altered

43.5   **for** sandstrewer happened to **read** sandstrewer
happening to
we reject HWG's TN and return to the ungrammatical
form of R–TS–1922, which we take to have been
deliberate

306.4   **for** less. Grinding **read** less ... Grinding
this is the first of twenty-five entries of '...' made by J in
proof (here in page proof, JJA 27 p. 36); HWG's reversion
to the full stops, etc., of R is rejected (v. his TN on
1404.28/1117.8)

358.10–11   **for** to. For **read** to ... for
entered by J in page proof (JJA 27 p. 38)

596.9–597.3   **delete** not turning a hair, +

612.14   **for** yes, ay or **read** yes, ay, or
J's correction in TS (JJA 15 p. 382) overrides R

666.2   **for** The Skibbereen father **read** The
                 Skibereen father
                 see 7–735 above; J also wrote one 'b' here in page proof
                 (JJA 27 p. 85)

682.5   **for** or. **read** or ...
                 entered by J in page proof (JJA 27 p. 86)

715.10–11   **for** not, your **read** not? **new paragraph** Your
                 R f.19 shows paragraph indent, confirmed by J when he
                 changed 'not,' to 'not?' in placards (JJA 20 p. 270)

768.10   **for** mean, and the **read** mean, the+

778.3–7   **delete** with a smile of unbelief+

899.11   **for** and then the **read** and the+

947.12   **for** in to the **read** in the
                 'to' (if it is 'to') appears to be deleted in R f.25

962.5   **for** and wreckers, the **read** and wrecks, the+

996.1   **for** was that colonel **read** was colonel+

1090.13   **for** exactly. **read** exactly ...
                 J wrote '...' in page proof (JJA 27 p. 97)

1103.5–8   **delete** in the next house+

1112.2–3   **for** blood, from some bump **read** blood,
                 bump+

1117.8, 1118.4,7 **for** probably and [...] others in case they.
                 read probably ... and [...] others ... in case
                 they ...
                 J entered '...' in all five places in this and the next entry, in
                 placards (JJA 20 p. 317)

225

1125.15, 1126.14	**for** any because […] are. But **read** any … because […] are … But see 16–1117, 1118 above
1221.3	**for** small. Intellectual **read** small … Intellectual entered by J in page proof (JJA 27 p. 100)
1247.8–13	**delete** Or a change of address anyway.+
1281.2–1282.1	**delete** *Sceptre* a shade heavier, 5 to 4 on *Zinfandel*, 20 to 1 *Throwaway* (off).+ cf TN
1417.2	**for** many. **read** many … J wrote '…' on placards (as an original draft, not an emendation, JJA 20 p. 340)
1424.2	**for** he. **read** he … entered by J in page proof (JJA 27 p. 104)
1448.6	**for** the. He **read** the … He entered by J in page proof (JJA 27 p. 123)
1458.6	**for** he so **read** he … so entered by J here (and in the next three entries) in placards (JJA 20 p. 359)
1462.7	**for** storm. And **read** storm … And see 16–1458 above
1470.9	**for** he? I **read** he? … I see 16–1458 above
1478.10	**for** him yet **read** him … yet see 16–1458 above
1482.6	**for** of gutterpress about **read** of letterpress about+

1513.9–11	**for** (Parnell's) a silk one was **read** (Parnell's) was+
1564.7	**for** of complimentplaying and **read** of complimentpaying and J wrote 'complimentplaying' in R (f. 42), but this was misread by the typist as 'compliment paying', which J then joined up in placards to make one word (JJA 20 p. 361); accept the later version
1612.10	**for** alternatives. Everything **read** alternatives ... Everything entered by J in placards (JJA 20 p. 361)
1614.6,10	**for** was he was a shade standoffish **read** was that he was a bit standoffish this is J's repair of the result of a typist's error (placards, JJA 20 p. 362); it's a coherent second thought, so keep it
1629.5–9	**delete** where age was no bar+
1636.5	**for** let x equal **read** let X equal we read this as cap 'X', not l.c. 'x' (R f.45)
1637.12	**for** his gentle repartee **read** his repartee+
1646.6–9	**delete** Do you like cocoa?+
1649.6	**for** to. **read** to ... entered by J in placards (JJA 20 p. 362)
1651.12	**for** less. **read** less ... entered by J in placards (JJA 20 p. 362)
1654.2–1655.3	**for** billing, concert tours in English watering resorts packed with hydros and seaside theatres, **read** billing, hydros and concert tours in English watering resorts packed with theatres,+ the recasting of the phrases in R (f. 45) is perfectly clear and presumably deliberate; reject TN

1661.11   **for** to. **read** to ...
entered by J in placards (JJA 20 p. 363)

1707.6,8   **for** moment, the door. **read** moment ... the door to ...
entered by J in placards (JJA 20 p. 364) and page proofs (JJA 27 p. 132) respectively

1719.14   **delete** Come.+

1757.6   **for** he had heard **read** he heard+

1761.7–8   **for** didn't sing it but **read** didn't but+

1763.12   **for** who *annos ludendo* **read** who *anno ludendo*
retain J's clearly-written '*anno*' (R f. 49) and reject HWG's emendation (v. TN)

1799.10   **for** old. **read** old ...
entered by J in placards (JJA 20 p. 366)

1804.14   **for** usual handsome blackguard **read** usual blackguard+

1805.7   **for** an insatiable hankering **read** an indubitable hankering
R (f. 51) reads 'insatiable', but TS (JJA 15 p. 401) mistakenly reads 'indubitable'; whereupon J adds 'unquestionably' to TS, presumably as a deliberate tautology; retain 'indubitable'

1839.14   **for** have. Added **read** have ... Added
J wrote '...' on placards (JJA 20 p. 370)

1866.5–6   **for** then. And **read** then ... And
entered by J in placards (JJA 20 p. 369)

17: Ithaca

Status TS copied from R, then revised and retyped before being set in type

5.13   **for** street: then, **read** street, north: then,
repairing a compositor's omission in placards (JJA 21 p.
3), J recast this sequence with the additional 'north'; retain
the later version

70.2   **for** What act did **read** What action did
J wrote 'action' in R (f.1), but in page proof (JJA 27 p.
140) the second half of the word was marked with a cross;
the printer deleted the whole word, Joyce did not see
corrected proof, and 'action' was reinstated in p1E – reject
HWG's 'act'

98.13   **for** Roman indiction 2, **read** Roman indication
2,
despite HWG's TN, we see no reason not to follow J's
clear inscription in page proof (JJA 27 p. 140) of
'indication' here, and of 'MXMIV' in the next line; reject
HWG's emendations

99.4   **for** 6617, MCMIV. **read** 6617, MXMIV.
see 17–98 above

165.10   **for** of filter mains **read** of filtre mains
'filtre', which is entered by J as a correction in placards
(JJA 21 p. 7), is given by OED as an alternative spelling of
'filter' through the 19th century; retain, and reject HWG's
TN

528.6–7   **for** and about **read** and Bloom's thoughts
about
HWG's version follows page proof (JJA 27 p. 155, which
is not in fact the 'simplest reciprocal form' of the question,
which would require the deletion of 'about', 528.7); but in
any case J's revision in the autograph Errata supersedes the
earlier reading

752.4   **for** exegetical, homiletic, toponomastic, **read**
exegetical, homilectic, toponomastic,
'homiletic' is HWG's emendation for J's incorrect but
clearly written 'homilectic' (page proof, JJA 27 p. 161)

801.9   **for** legend. **read** legend?
J wrote 'legend?' (R f.²7) and it went all the way through –
reject HWG's emendation

966.12   **for** the Ship hotel **read** the *Ship* hotel
J's italics (R f.12) – keep them

1202.3   **for** sanitariness, pilosity. To **read** sanitariness,
pelosity. To
'pelosity' is J's spelling (R f. 16); reject HWG's
emendation

1203.1   **no new line at** To Stephen:
there is no convincing indication of a new line in R f.16

1472.6   **for** Chocolate 0–1–0 **read** Chocolate 0–0–1
see 17–1476 below

1476.2   **for** Balance 0–16–6 **read** Balance 0–17–5
somehow the clearly-written '0.1.0' (TS, JJA 16 p. 132)
was changed by the first placard (JJA 21 p. 89) to the
more realistic '0.0.1' (Bloom could hardly have stuffed a
shilling's-worth of plain chocolate, together with bread,
into a sidepocket, 15–143), and J adjusted the balance in
the autograph Errata to fit – reject HWG's return to R and
his TN (in which, incidentally, HWG wrongly argues that
Bloom would have only the 'balance' of 16/6 – or 17/5 – in
his pocket, not adding the 'cash in hand' of 4/9, making
totals of £1/1/3 or £1/2/2)

1491.6   **for** lacerated ungual fragment. **read** lacerated
unguical fragment.
'unguical' (p1E) is given by OED as a rare alternative form
of 'ungual' – reject HWG's emendation

1494.1   **for** other ungual fragments, **read** other
unguical fragments,
see 17–1491 above

1782.8   **for** Mr + Mrs **read** Mr & Mrs
we read the sign in R (f.17) as an ampersand, not a plus
sign

1800.1   **for** alphabetic boustrophedonic punctated
          read alphabetic boustrephodontic punctated
          although doubly wrong, 'boustrephodontic' is J's spelling
          (JJA 27 p. 195, partially corrected in 1932); reject HWG's
          emendation

1875.5   **for** of Rudolf Virag **read** of Rudolph Virag
          J wrote Rudolph (R f.20), which should be retained (cf.
          17–1869.2 and TN), even though the spelling 'Rudolf' had
          been used by Virag in 1852; reject HWG's emendation

1958.4   **for** rendered departure not **read** rendered it
          not
          J altered 'it' to 'departure' in pencil in R (f.23) after it had
          been typed at 17–1958.4 and 17–1962.4, but not at
          17–1968.4 (which is HWG's emendation); the alteration
          was not made in proof and should be ignored

1962.4   **for** rendered departure not **read** rendered it
          not
          see 17–1958 above

1968.4   **for** rendered departure desirable? **read**
          rendered it desirable?
          see 17–1958 above

2180.13   **for** not so calamitous **read** not as calamitous
          J originally wrote 'so' (R f.28), but when the word was
          accidentally dropped he replaced it with 'as' (placards, JJA
          21 p. 126); keep the later version

18: Penelope

Status TS copied from R

124.9   **for** his fathers I **read** his father I
          HWG's TN is persuasive; J may have intended 'fathers' as
          a genitive, but he changed it to 'father' in TS (JJA 16 p.
          303), perhaps because he thought that a reader would take
          'fathers' for a plural; accept his alteration

444.3 **for** and kicked up **read** and kick up
J wrote 'kick' (placards, JJA 21 p. 248) and may have
intended Molly to make the error of tense here – reject
HWG's emendation

579.15 **for** the 1 half **read** the one half
correcting a typist's error, J wrote 'one' in TS (JJA 16 p.
316), not '1' as in R – keep the later version

617.6–11 **for** sing Waiting and in old Madrid Concone
read sing in old Madrid or Waiting Concone
correcting an omission in TS (JJA 16 p. 317, cf. R f.10
and 9ᵛ), J used a new wording with a slightly different
meaning – keep the later version

723.10 **for** the piannyer that **read** the pyannyer that
J wrote 'piannyer' in R (f. 11ᵛ), but later corrected a
typist's error to 'pyannyer' (placards, JJA 21 p. 14); keep
the later version

908.8 **for** pianissimo eeeee one **read** pianissimo
eeeeeee one
there are 5 'e's in R f.15 but J, correcting a typist's error
on TS (JJA 16 p. 326), changed it to 8 'e's – keep the later
version

1333.6 **for** a potent professor **read** a patent professor
we read J's entry in placards (JJA 21 p. 303) as 'patent',
not 'potent'